Hard Roads Home

Also by Peter Stitt

The World's Hieroglyphic Beauty

Uncertainty and Plenitude

James Wright: The Heart of the Light
(edited, with Frank Graziano)

Hard Roads Home
How I Found a Family in Mormonia

Peter Stitt

952 Frederick Street | Hagerstown MD 21740

Hard Roads Home: How I Found a Family in Mormonia.

For information address Somondoco Press,
P.O. Box 1014, Shepherdstown, WV 25443.
www.somondocopress.com

First Edition

Printed in the Unites States of America.

ISBN 978-0-9789617-7-0

Book design by Brandon Cornwell, HBP Inc.

This book is dedicated to my Four Muses

Sheila Mulligan

Melanie Webb

Crystal Webb

Rebekkah Webb

Contents

Part XIV
Emma and Sheila

Part XV
Polygamy and Monogamy

Acknowledgments

Illustrations by Dale Gallon

Hard Roads Home

Part I
Settings Out

I Discover The Book of Mormon

January, 2000, the third. I was stopped for the night, finally. I had found a motel in WaKeeny, Kansas, the Kansas Kountry Inn, a mom-and-pop motel maybe a mile from the bridge where I had skidded into the railing and damaged the front end of my car.

I threw my bag on the bed and looked around. I saw a nightstand. In the drawer of the nightstand I found three books: a Gideon's Bible, a phone book, The Book of Mormon. I thought of Rocky Raccoon.

> Rocky Raccoon
> Stepped into his room
> Only to find Gideon's Bible.
> …
> Gideon checked out
> And he left it no doubt
> To help with good Rocky's revival.

Rocky's revival? What about my revival? I opened Gideon's Bible. It was King James's Bible. I had read King James's Bible. I pulled out the phone book. I called the night number for the B and C Body Shop and talked to a woman named Cindy. She told me to come on over in the morning. Terry, her husband, would do what he could to get me back on the road.

I was on the lam. I was on my way to a new life. Things had gone bad, personal things. Love had died. Sometimes love dies. It can happen to anyone. It is a sad thing, a tragic thing. I had to get away. I had left for good.

I was on my way to Mexico. I was on my way to Utah. I was on my way to Mexico by way of Salt Lake City, Utah. Sheila was in Salt Lake City, in the land of the Mormons, in the capital of The Kingdom of Moroni. Sheila and her children, the three adopted girls.

I climbed into bed. I opened the third book, The Book of Mormon. I started at the beginning. I read the "Introduction," I read "The Testimony of Eight Witnesses," I read the "Testimony of the Prophet Joseph Smith." I started reading The Book of Mormon itself. It seemed like the right thing to do, stranded for the night between wives.

I had left Jean. I was on my way to Sheila. I would visit her for a week and then go on to Mexico. I would stay in Mexico for three months, alone. I would make sure my head was screwed on tight. I would try to be sure of what I was doing.

A Family Scene

January 2002, two years later. A Sunday morning in Pennsylvania. We are at home, in the house we call the Pond House. Crystal is practicing the viola. Sheila is sweeping the stairs. Melanie is painting her model of a hot-air balloon. Rebekkah is playing Nintendo.

Both doors to the dining room are shut. "No," says Sheila from downstairs. "No one is allowed in there. Melanie is doing her project."

I am upstairs, in my home office, working on my project, writing about the family, writing about the Mormons.

The "Testimony of the Prophet Joseph Smith"

1823. Joseph Smith was seventeen years old. He worked hard all day in the fields with his father, Joseph Smith, Senior. They were farmers, farmers and gold diggers. Gold digging was a big deal at that time in their part of the world, in upstate New York, the town of Palmyra. No one ever found any gold, but everyone knew it was out there. Lots of it. It was buried somewhere, lots of somewheres. The gold diggers had seer stones. They would look into their seer stones and see where the gold was buried. They would go there and dig it up. They never found any gold. People paid them money to do this.

It was a time of religious fervor. People believed in things they could not hear, smell, taste, touch, or see. They believed in buried gold. They believed in angels and gods. Joseph believed in buried gold. He believed in angels and gods. He believed in Jesus. God and Jesus had visited him when he was fourteen years old, in 1820. They had told him not to join any existing church. They had told him to prepare himself for an important task.

Now Joseph was seventeen. 1823, the twenty-first of September, the day of the autumnal equinox. He went to bed. In his "Testimony" he recalled, "I betook myself to prayer and supplication to Almighty God." Joseph was a reader of the Bible. He knew the language of the Bible. He knew the word *betook*.

As he was praying in his bed, a light appeared in the room. It became brighter and "continued to increase until the room was brighter than at noonday." "A personage appeared" at Joseph's bedside, "standing in the air," wearing "a loose robe of exquisite whiteness. It was a whiteness beyond anything earthly that I had ever seen."

The robe did not cover the whole personage. His "hands were naked, and his arms also, a little above the wrists; so, also, were his feet naked, as were his legs, a little above the ankles." Joseph saw that the personage's "head and neck were also bare." He saw "that [the personage] had no other clothing on but this robe, as it was open, so that I could see into his bosom." This the testimony of Joseph.

The personage spoke, "called me by name." He "said unto me that he was a messenger sent from the presence of God to me."

The personage was an angel and "his name was Moroni." He was the son of Mormon. He said "that God had a work for me to do."

He "said there was a book deposited, written upon gold plates." The book was buried on a hill, the hill Cumorah, in the neighborhood of Joseph's father's farm. Moroni said "that the fullness of the everlasting Gospel was contained in" the book; "there were also two stones in silver bows...fastened to a breastplate..., the Urim and Thummim.... God had prepared [the stones] for the purpose of translating the book."

Joseph knew about stones. He had looked into stones and seen buried gold, buried gold that was not there.

The light gathered itself. "A conduit [appeared] right up into heaven," and Moroni "ascended until he entirely disappeared." The room was dark again. Joseph trembled alone in his bed. Then the light returned and Moroni "again related the very same things which he had done at his first visit, without the least variation." Moroni again ascended, then returned and repeated the whole performance a third time.

Maybe Moroni was dumb. Maybe he twice forgot he had already visited Joseph. Maybe Moroni thought Joseph was dumb. Maybe he thought he had to tell him again and then again. Maybe Moroni just wanted to see Joseph again and then again.

In The Book of Mormon there are some paintings. The painting of Joseph shows a handsome young man with sensual lips and wavy hair. His eyes are full and dark. They gaze into the middle distance off to the viewer's left. The painting of the angel Moroni shows a rugged, handsome, middle-aged man wearing bracelets, trousers, and a brown cloak. His arms and neck are bare. I cannot see into his bosom.

Moroni is kneeling in the woods, beside a tree. It is winter. Snow of an exquisite whiteness lies upon the ground. Moroni kneels in the snow and his breath makes steam. His head is tilted upward, and his eyes are closed in prayer. His bare, muscular arms extend forward and down. His clasped hands rest upon a bundle of thin gold

The Angel Moroni

plates bound together with red twine. Dirt surrounds a perfectly rectangular hole that has been chopped into the frozen ground. A sword protrudes from the ground near Moroni's right hand. Moroni's arms are bare and muscular. He has a terrific tan. Veins bulge up from beneath the skin of his bare arms. This angel has powerful hormones.

Gold plates were buried. Stones were buried with the gold plates. The stones were named Urim and Thummim. The stones were fastened to a breastplate with silver bows. A book was written on the gold plates. The stones were for translating the book. Joseph was to find the plates and translate the book. The book was written by Mormon and delivered by Moroni. Joseph was to be Mormon's prophet. Joseph was to found the Kingdom of Moroni.

The Day of My Fleeing

I left home on the second day of January, 2000, the second day of the millennium, bound for Mexico, to stay three months in the condo owned by my wife and her family. I had been there before, a year earlier, for six weeks, in the winter. Alone. I had not wanted to be alone, but Jean would not join me, I knew not why. I did not want to go alone this year, but again she would not join me, and again I knew not why.

We had argued about it the year before. Argued by e-mail, I writing from Mexico, she writing from our home in Gettysburg. She would complain about the ice and the snow: "The sidewalks are completely iced over. I don't know how to clear them."

"Why try? It is warm down here, sunny. I walk on the beach, I watch the pelicans, I swim with the dolphins. We can afford the airfare. I can pick you up in Guaymas."

"No," she said. She had no reason to stay in Pennsylvania, none that I could see. But every time I asked her please to join me, she said no.

I knew I would be returning the next year. For a longer stay, because of my sabbatical, because of my release from spring semester teaching. I wanted her there with me. Marriage means being together, I thought. Maybe not all the time, not every minute of every day, but for sure if the couple could spend the winter months together in Mexico, away from the ice and the cold.

Periodically I would ask again. All through 1999, at least once a month, I would say we needed to go together. "Come with me this time. Why stay here in the cold and the ice and the snow?"

The best answer I got was "maybe." "Maybe I will come." Eventually I grew tired of hearing "maybe." I grew tired of hearing it at home, tired of hearing it during marriage counseling.

By November, *I* had gotten involved. The character I call *I*. The other side of me. Eventually *I* scratched a line between us, between her and me. "Come with me or it is over," *I* said. "This is getting ridiculous. Come with me to Mexico, or the marriage is over." I was getting angry, angrier.

She still said "maybe." She said, "I won't come now, but maybe I will join you later." I went alone. I and *I* went to Mexico alone. To Salt Lake City and then on to Mexico. We were not coming back.

I left at about noon. I drove across Pennsylvania and part of Ohio. I listened to the radio, listened to CDs. One song among many caught in my mind, Paul Simon's song, "America." The speaker, the singer, is on a bus, riding across America. He is with someone, but he is also alone. This is how the song ends:

> "Kathy, I'm lost," I said, though I knew she was sleeping
> I'm empty and aching and I don't know why
> Counting the cars on the New Jersey Turnpike,
> They've all gone to look for America.

He is empty and aching, lost, while "Kathy" sleeps on. He speaks, but she does not hear. He is with her, but he is alone. He is on the road, crossing America.

Joseph Visits the Hill Cumorah

In her biography of Joseph Smith, *No Man Knows My History*, Fawn Brodie describes Moroni's nighttime visit to Joseph. She says, "to be authentic, celestial truth must be thrice repeated." Moroni visited Joseph three times that night. Now I know why.

The next day, Joseph was working in the fields with his father. He became exhausted and pale, and his father sent him home to be doctored. Joseph headed toward home but lost consciousness and fell to the ground while trying to climb a fence. Moroni suddenly appeared in a beam of bright light, repeated his message a fourth time, and told Joseph to tell his father.

Joseph returned to the field and told his father about the visions, his father the gold digger. Perhaps Joseph, Senior, stroked his chin and said, "Hmm. You say the plates are gold?"

Joseph went to the hill, the Hill Cumorah. Beneath a large stone he found the gold plates, the breastplate, and the seer stones, Urim and Thummim. As he reached down toward them, Moroni appeared again and said, "No." He said it in a voice of thunder. He knew that Joseph was thinking of the gold and said Joseph had to wait. He had to prove himself worthy. Maybe he could have the plates in four years. Moroni would stay in touch. They might do lunch.

Moroni returned each year on the same day, the twenty-first of September. Then in 1827 Moroni said, "OK." He said Joseph could get the plates now. Joseph went to the hill and moved the stone. He removed the plates.

Perhaps Joseph went straight home with the plates. Perhaps he was first accosted by a hostile spirit. Eber D. Howe, author of *Mormonism Unvailed* [sic] (1834), had heard two stories. In one of them Joseph set the plates on the ground, looked into the hole, and "saw a toad, which immediately transformed itself into a spirit, and gave [Joseph] a tremendous blow."

In the other story "a spirit assaulted [Joseph] with the intention of getting [the plates] from his possession." This would be a bad spirit. The spirit "actually jerked them out of [Joseph's] hands," but "Joe, nothing daunted, in return seized them again, and started to run." Then "his Satanic Majesty (or the spirit) applied his foot to the Prophet's seat of honor, which raised him three or four feet from the ground."

Perhaps Joseph hit the ground running.

Writers at Work I

I had been there before, Salt Lake City, at a writers' conference. Six months earlier, in July, in 1999, for a week. I was there as a visiting editor and writer. Alone, though I had invited Jean, who said no. Another time she did not want to travel. She flew to Arizona for six weeks instead.

I was working hard, doing panels, conferring with student writers, attending readings and talks. The conference was held on the campus of a college, Westminster College, on the eastern edge of the city.

The faculty was housed in a dormitory, and everyone had a roommate. My roommate was Lawrence. He was from Salt Lake City and knew a lot of the people attending the conference. On the first night he and I and some of those others had dinner at a grocery store in a shopping center close to the college. The grocery store was called Wild Oats, and the food was organic. We ordered from the deli and sat at a table.

Several times each day I would walk between the dormitory and the rest of the campus, and each time I had to cross a bridge. Beneath the bridge was a creek, a beautiful creek, a powerful mountain stream.

Another night I was alone at dinner time. I remembered seeing restaurants in the shopping area near the grocery store. Since it was close, I decided to walk there. I was not sure of the direction, so I decided to follow the creek upstream, up the hill, toward the east. Maybe it would be the wrong direction, but I would have the creek for company.

I followed the creek for half a block, and then it disappeared. It disappeared by coming out of a pipe. Someone had buried the creek. So I followed the pipe by following what used to be the bed of the creek. I followed the low ground and the trees. Mostly

I had to do this by walking on neighborhood streets. Occasionally the creek would emerge by running into a pipe, and then I would follow the creek itself until it disappeared again, disappeared by coming out of a pipe.

The neighborhood was leafy, orderly. The grass in the yards was green, the trees were mature. I guessed that the houses had been built in the twenties and thirties. I thought of Frank Lloyd Wright. I thought of the Prairie style, brick and wood, one storey with strong horizontal lines, a high basement, a shallow attic, porches and leaded glass. Strong, stable, solid, orderly houses.

The streets were straight, except for the ones twisted by the creek. The blocks were long. Order had been imposed. I liked the neighborhood. I liked Salt Lake City. I looked for Wild Oats. I looked for the shopping center. I did not find them. I found a Starbuck's. I found a piece of lemon poppy-seed pound cake. I found a cup of coffee.

Later I learned more about the creek. It was called Emigration Creek, by the Mormons, the Mormons who had founded Salt Lake City. The Mormons had immigrated into the valley by following that creek, so they named it Emigration Creek. Later they had buried it. The Mormons had buried Emigration Creek.

The Mormons buried all the creeks in Salt Lake City. The Mormons are an orderly people, and the creeks were disorderly. The creeks ran all over the place and were prone to flooding, so the Mormons buried the creeks. The Mormons wanted an orderly world. The Mormons wanted a clean world. A strong, stable, solid, orderly, clean world.

Joseph Translates the Book

Joseph sat behind a screen with his face in a hat and translated the book. The stones Urim and Thummim were in the hat with Joseph's face. The stones glowed, and the words of the translation appeared upon them. When Joseph was not working on the plates, he hid them in a box in the woods.

As Joseph spoke the words aloud, Emma sat at a table on the

Joseph Smith

other side of the screen and wrote them down. Emma was Joseph's wife and scribe, the first of many wives, the first of many scribes.

No one but Joseph ever saw the plates. Some of the scribes and many other people wanted to see the plates, but Joseph would not show them. Eventually Joseph understood that he had to show the plates. He took three people into the woods and opened the box. The witnesses looked into the box and saw that it was empty.

Joseph sat them down and made them pray. He kept them praying for hours. He harangued them with prayer. They looked into the box again, now with "spiritual sight," and saw that the plates were there. Right there in the box where they had always been.

Later other people doubted that there were plates. Joseph gathered up eight trustworthy people, eight witnesses. He gathered his father, two of his brothers, four neighbors named Whitmer, and a man named Hiram Page. Joseph took them into the woods and harangued them with prayer. They looked into the box with spiritual sight and saw that the plates were there. They returned to town and signed a statement, "The Testimony of Eight Witnesses." When Mark Twain read the statement, he said, "I could not feel more satisfied and at rest if the entire Whitmer family had testified."

The Book of Mormon was published in 1830, in Palmyra, on the twenty-sixth of March. On the sixth of April of that year and in that town, Joseph founded the Church of Jesus Christ of Latter-day Saints, with six members: his mother, his father, his brothers, and two neighbors. The neighbors may have been Whitmers.

Writers at Work II

On my way to an evening reading the second night of the conference, I was approached by a woman clutching a book. "Are you Peter Stitt?" she asked.

"Yes."

"I'm Sheila Mulligan. You published a story of mine in *The Gettysburg Review* a couple of years ago, 'Dressing Estelle.'"

"Oh, yes, a really good story," I said, pretending to remember.

"I bought your book. Would you sign it for me?"

"I would love to," I said, patting my pockets. "I don't have a pen. Do you have one?"

She looked in her purse. "I must have one in here somewhere. Oh, darn, I guess not. Maybe you can sign it tomorrow."

"Yeah, OK, that sounds good." She turned and started to walk away. "Wait, I said. Aren't you going to the reading?"

"Yes, I thought it was time to go in now."

"Maybe you will sit with me. Not in the same chair, of course, ha ha."

"OK."

It was not a good reading. As we left the theatre, Sheila was walking ahead of me. I glanced away for a moment, then turned back. I saw her disappearing through the crowd.

We ran into each other the next day. And the next. And the next. I found out why she had left so abruptly after that reading. She had a husband and three adopted children at home. Her in-laws were visiting. She needed to get right home.

I also found out about the pen. The pen she could not find in her purse. It was a ploy. When I said I did not have a pen, she decided she did not have one either.

The Start of the Movement West

Joseph Smith was not a prophet in his homeland. Thrice had he been tried for fraud, once convicted, because of his gold-digging schemes. Now he was hawking a new religion, born of gold-digging. His father-in-law, Isaac Hale, had watched Joseph translating the plates. Later he testified to what he had seen: "I conscientiously believe…that the whole 'Book of Mormon' (so called) is a silly fabrication of falsehood and wickedness, got up for speculation, and with a design to dupe the credulous and unwary—and in order that its fabricators may live upon the spoils of those who swallow the deception."

The next January, 1831, nine months after the founding of the church in Palmyra, Joseph fled what had become a place of doubt, suspicion, contention, disbelief. He took his family and his flock westward, to Kirtland, Ohio, to his first Zion, his first holy city, a place of sanctity, of sanctuary. A place where a prophet could pursue his dream unhindered.

In Kirtland he converted all the members of Sidney Rigdon's Campbellite cult to Mormonism. By autumn he had sent a party of converts off to Missouri, to Independence, to establish a Mormon colony farther west. In March 1832, he and Rigdon were tarred and feathered for causing trouble in Hiram, Ohio, I am not sure why. Rigdon was a tough guy, a blowhard, and Joseph was a schemer. They may have had a money scam going.

The persecution of Mormons in Missouri commenced in 1833. Joseph led an armed party west in 1834, then returned to Kirtland. Joseph and Rigdon tried to open a bank, but were denied a license. They formed an "anti-banking society" and issued a bunch of paper money, trading it for goods. Later they refused to redeem the paper money. Rigdon was jailed and brought to trial.

In January 1838, Joseph and Rigdon fled, three steps ahead of the law, from Kirtland to Far West, Missouri. The remainder of the flock followed in July. The troubles in Missouri had already gone from bad to worse.

A Week in Salt Lake City

I stayed two months in Mexico, alone, asking myself a question, thinking about love, about the death of love, about where love goes when it dies. I thought maybe to Mexico, maybe to Utah. I thought maybe it just hits the road.

In February I visited Salt Lake City and stayed in a motel for a week. On the Wednesday night, I wanted to watch a basketball game that was not on regular TV. I asked the guy at the motel desk about a sports bar. "Good luck in this town," he said. He called a taxi for me and suggested that I ask the cabbie.

The cabbie chuckled. "You've got one option," he said. "Mormons don't believe in drinking, so there are no public bars. They have to be private clubs. I know one downtown that might have your game."

I could not get in without a membership card. "Someone who is already a member has to sponsor you," the hostess said. "We don't take strangers."

I went out and talked to a drunk leaning on a lamppost. He agreed to be my sponsor. The hostess accepted my five-dollar membership fee, made a copy of my ID, and told me to have a nice time.

The only TV showing the game was in a far corner of the basement. A waitress named Tiffany brought me a beer and some chicken wings. About halfway through the game, a couple sat down at the table next to mine. They drank beer and talked.

I had another beer, maybe a third. When the game was almost over, the woman at the other table put on her jacket and left. The guy sat there a while, then stood up and started to put on his own jacket. Something heavy and metal fell out of a pocket and clattered on the floor. It was a handgun, an automatic, a nine millimeter or a forty-five.

The basement got real quiet. The guy said, "Shit," picked up the gun, put it in his pocket, sat back down. I looked at the TV. The game was over. Duke had beaten Carolina by two points.

I noticed three guys making their way through the room, big guys. One kept to the far wall, one kept to the near wall, and one walked down the middle of the room, between the tables. They converged on the guy with the gun.

They talked for a while, four guys in a sports bar on a Wednesday night, the big guys standing, the other guy in his chair. Then the guy with the gun stood up, and they left together.

As I paid for my beers, I chatted with Tiffany. She said the three big guys were bouncers. The other guy had claimed to be a cop. I said, "Some cop."

Tiffany said, "Maybe he was, maybe he wasn't. Maybe it doesn't matter."

I looked at her for a moment, then asked, "Why do you say that?"

"You don't want to mess with the cops," she said. "Not here. Not in Salt Lake City."

I went back to the motel. At the end of the week I went back to Mexico.

The Color White

The Mormons drive white cars. The Mormons call themselves saints. The Mormons call everyone else gentiles. The gentiles in Salt Lake City call the Mormons the LDS, short for the Latter-day Saints. The gentiles of Salt Lake City say things like, "That's an LDS thing." The white cars of Salt Lake City are an LDS thing. Salt Lake City is overrun by white cars.

Moroni appeared to Joseph in white, a robe of exquisite whiteness. White is the color of purity. White is the color of sanctity. White is the color of orderliness. White is the color of control. White can be the absence of color.

The saints wear white shirts. The saints wear white underwear. The saints have white appliances. White is an LDS thing. White cars are an LDS thing.

The LDS do not drive white cars because of the sun, to keep their cars cool in the summer. That would be a gentile thing. The LDS drive white cars because of Joseph and Moroni. Joseph and Moroni are an LDS thing. White is an LDS thing. White is an orderly thing.

Part II

Doctrines and Domicile

Crystal Webb

A Conflict with Crystal

Today is Tuesday, a Tuesday morning in June 2002. 6:15 a.m. I am back in my home office, working on my project, writing about the Mormons, writing about the family. I have just had a conversation with Crystal. A conversation about *messy* and *neat*, about rooms that are messy and neat, about her room.

Her room used to be all messy. Today it is mostly messy and somewhat neat. I was urging her toward neat. She was urging me toward messy, toward understanding messy. Toward understanding that messy is a fact of life, a fact of children's rooms. I am to chill. I am to take a chill pill. She is to clean her room. She is to pick up a banana peel and put it in the trash.

We are having a conflict, a fatherly-daughterly conflict. A conflict as gentle as such conflicts get. The character I call *I* is playing no role. I am being I, and Crystal is being Crystal. We do not raise our voices. We do not make demands. We offer suggestions.

Neither of us is much worried about how the conflict will turn out. We know that it will turn out OK. I will give a little, and she will give a little. The room will be clean enough to satisfy us both. That seems good to me, a good way to approach conflict.

The Mormons did not approach conflict that way. The world surrounding the Mormons did not approach conflict that way. The world in general does not approach conflict that way. No one ever said the world was perfect. I am not saying that now.

The Doctrines of Mormonism I

Joseph Smith was in direct contact with God. Joseph would come up against a problem while inventing and administering his religion. He would consult with God about the problem, and God would give him the solution. Joseph would call his flock together and announce his revelation. The revelations of God to Joseph Smith constitute the doctrines of Mormonism.

The best summary of those early doctrines was written by Judge John Cradlebaugh and delivered to the United States Congress in 1863. Some years earlier, not long after the Mountain Meadows Massacre, President James Buchanan had sent Cradlebaugh to Utah to investigate rumors of violence and lawless behavior said to be part of Mormon belief. In his report to Congress and the president, Cradlebaugh wrote:

> Mormonism…preaches openly that the more wives and children its men have in this world, the purer, more influential and conspicuous will they be in the next; that wives, children, and property will not only be restored, but doubled in the resurrection. It adopts the use of prayers and baptism for the dead, as a part of its creed. Mormons claim to be favored with marvelous gifts—the power of speaking in tongues, of casting out devils, of curing the sick, and of healing the lame and the halt. They claim that they have a living prophet, seer and revelator who holds the keys of the Kingdom of Heaven, and through whose intercession alone access can be had. They recognize the Bible, but they interpret it for themselves, and hold that it is subject to be changed by new revelation, which, they say, supersedes old revelation. One of their doctrines is that of continued progression to ultimate perfection. They say God was but a man, who went on developing and increasing until he reached his present high capacity; and they teach that Mormons will be equal to him; in a word, that good Mormons will become gods.

They teach the shedding of blood for remission of sins, or, in other words, if a Mormon apostatizes, his throat shall be cut, and his blood poured out upon the ground for the remission of his sins.... They claim that Mormonism is to go on spreading until it overthrows all the nations of the earth, and if necessary for its accomplishment, its success shall be consummated by the sword.

A Sunday Morning in Salt Lake City

I left the place in Mexico in early March and moved to Salt Lake City. I stayed a couple of weeks in a motel, then found an apartment. On a Sunday morning I left the motel early to find an ATM for money and a restaurant for breakfast. The ATM refused to give me money. After my fifth try it kept my card. My salary was deposited automatically every month into a joint account back home in Gettysburg. There should have been plenty of money, but I could not get any. "Shit," I muttered to myself, "shit fuck shit fuck shit." I was a little pissed.

As I drove away from the bank, I passed a cop getting back into his car after giving someone a ticket. He put on his lights and stopped me at the driveway to the restaurant. "Jesus fucking shit Christ," I muttered to myself, "what now?"

"License and registration, please." He was young, tall, muscular. He could have been a bouncer.

"What's the problem? I was going about two miles an hour."

"See that video camera pointing out the front window of my car? This stop is being taped. Do you have a problem with that?"

"No, but why did you stop me?"

"You don't have a front license plate." Great. First the ATM card, now a shit-for-brains cop.

"No kidding," I said. "I wonder if that is because my car is registered in Pennsylvania, where they don't have front plates."

He looked at me for a long moment. "Maybe that is so," he said. "But I see that the front of your car is also wrecked."

"Brilliant!" I said. "You notice everything! You must be the Cop of the Year."

"What did you say?"

"I said you are brilliant for noticing the damage to my car. First the front plate thing and now this! I said you should be named the Cop of the Year."

"I'm not a cop. I'm a police officer."

"Sorry. I meant Police Officer of the Year…your honor."

He gave me that cop stare for a moment. Then he sort of looked off into space, and his face brightened as he said, "Hey, the sergeant is going to be pleased when he looks at this tape. I've been on the force two and a half years. You're lucky I stopped you now. A year ago I would have already had you on the ground eating dirt with cuffs on your wrists. I'm making real progress here. The sergeant will love this tape."

He let me off with a warning.

The Doctrines of Mormonism II

The nineteenth-century doctrines of Mormonism were highly advantageous to Mormon men, men like Joseph Smith and his followers. The doctrines were financially rewarding and sexually rewarding. The doctrines of Mormonism were also tragic, potentially tragic. Because of the acceptance of violence, the doctrine of blood atonement.

A Mormon man got all the wives he wanted. His number of wives was doubled when he died. A Mormon man was encouraged to amass property. His property was doubled when he died. Heaven was full of wives and property. And children. The women took care of the children, the men took care of the wives and the property.

The doctrines of Mormonism were then and are still now exclusive. Mormonism is the only religion, the only true religion. Mormons are called saints. They are the only saints—everyone else is a gentile. Gentiles are not necessarily bad. They are basically nothing, nothing but souls awaiting conversion.

A gentile can be a gentile all his life. He can have only one wife or no wives, he can be dirt poor. He can be baptized posthumously, be made a member of the church, be inducted into the kingdom, all of this after he is dead and whether he wants it or not. Perhaps he will be given a heavenly mansion, a 401(k) and a factory, a cornfield or a farm, maybe a private airplane, maybe seventy-two virgin wives.

Mormonism wants him. Mormonism wants you. Mormonism intends to get you, living or dead.

Belle Wines

After a few weeks in motels, I found an unfurnished apartment in Salt Lake City, in a building called the Belle Wines. I bought a folding chair, a futon, and a bookcase. I found a table in an alley and used it as my desk. I piled my clothes on the floor in a closet and hung up my shirts.

I subscribed to a newspaper, the *Salt Lake City Tribune.* One week it featured a series of articles on the Mountain Meadows Massacre. In 1857 a large group of migrants on their way to California had been slaughtered in southern Utah, by the Mormons or by the Indians, the paper was not sure. Eventually a Mormon named John Doyle Lee was deemed responsible, tried, and executed. He may have been a scapegoat—other Mormons may have been involved; Brigham Young may have been involved; the Indians may have acted at the behest of the Mormons—but again the paper was not sure. The paper was not sure about a lot of things.

I read these articles in Salt Lake City, in the Kingdom of Moroni. Most readers of the *Salt Lake City Tribune* are practicing Mormons. I decided there was more to the story. I found the best bookstore in Salt Lake City, Sam Weller's, and bought a bunch of books. I bought Fawn Brodie's biography of Joseph Smith. I bought a book called *The Mountain Meadows Massacre,* by a Mormon woman named Juanita Brooks. Later I bought her biography of John Doyle Lee. Later still, when it was reissued after being out of print for years and years, I bought a copy of Lee's autobiography, *Mormonism Unveiled:*

The Confessions of John Doyle Lee.

I bought a lot of other books. I even tracked down a copy of Captain John Cook Bennett's scurrilous tome, *The History of the Saints*.

I got to know the city. I got to know the surrounding country, the mountains, the desert, the Great Salt Lake, the road from Salt Lake City to Wendover—Wendover, Utah, and West Wendover, Nevada—ninety miles away. The crew of the *Enola Gay* had trained for Hiroshima at the Wendover Air Force Base. I learned to play blackjack in the casinos in the Nevada part of Wendover.

Mormon Neighbors

Mormons make lousy neighbors. Mormons make good neighbors. Mormon neighbors can be both good and bad. At first Mormon neighbors seem all good. They are law-abiding and orderly. They stick together and want to be gentle. They want to be loved.

Wallace Stegner got this side of the Mormons right. "These people belong to one another, to a faith. They stand facing the rest of the world like a herd of rather amiable musk oxen, horns out, in a protective ring, watchful but not belligerent—full of confidence but ready to be reasonable, and wanting to be liked."

Mormons today are good neighbors. They are clean, they wear white shirts and white underwear, they drive white cars. Mostly they are good neighbors, but they can be irritating. They have many ideas for how gentiles can improve their lives. The lives of the Mormons cannot be improved.

In nineteenth-century America, the Mormons were lousy neighbors. Maybe they started out OK, but then they turned bad.

On the American frontier, in Missouri, they became lousy neighbors. They bought the best land, they grew the best crops, they built the nicest houses, they ran the best stores, they did business only with one another, they voted as a bloc. They had the most wives.

Eventually they made people angry, angered the gentiles, angered the other settlers. Wallace Stegner: "One way and another, the Mormons managed to get on ill terms with anyone, given time."

Because they could be so irritating, the Mormons were hounded, mistreated, persecuted, thrown out of their homes and off their land. They were beaten and stabbed, murdered and executed and slaughtered. Sometimes the Mormons were slaughtered in the coldest of blood.

Eventually the Mormons exacted revenge. They did not get even, but they exacted revenge.

The Capital City of the Kingdom of Moroni

My apartment was downtown, in the old part of Salt Lake City, an area of wide streets and large blocks. Soon after the Mormons arrived in 1847, Brigham Young laid out the town, on flat desert land just west of the Wasatch Range of the Rocky Mountains. He said that there should be one hundred fourteen blocks of ten acres each. One block would contain the temple and another would be Brigham's own, for his home and for the office he would use to run the colony.

The other blocks would be divided into eight lots of one and one-quarter acres each. One house only could be built on each lot, twenty feet back from the street fronting the property, two houses to each side of the block. The blocks would be square, with empty land for gardens in the middle. The streets would be broad, one hundred thirty-two feet across, so that a wagon with a team of oxen could be easily turned around.

The streets in that part of town are still one hundred thirty-two feet wide, giving the city a remarkable feeling of openness. Most of the blocks have been filled in—mews-like streets penetrate to many of the interiors—and a block with no apartment houses or stores and only eight standing houses is rare indeed. But the original layout is still perceptible, and the sense of geographic and urban order remains strong. The police have a lot to do with this.

Independence

Few episodes in American religious history parallel the barbarism of the

anti-Mormon persecutions. That the town in which these began should bear the name of Independence only accentuates the tragic irony of the case. Intermittently for thirteen years burnings and pillaging hounded the Mormons wherever they tried to settle in the Mississippi Valley, until it seemed there was something inevitable in the terrorism that bloodied their trail.
                                                                —Fawn M. Brodie

Mormonism, the Church of Jesus Christ of Latter-day Saints, grew. Many gentiles were converted. Mormonism moved. The Mormons wore out their welcome and moved, from New York to Ohio, Palmyra to Kirtland. They moved from Ohio to Missouri, Kirtland to Independence, to near Independence, Missouri. They had found Eden. They had found their Zion.

Their neighbors on the Missouri frontier were a rough crowd, luckhunters, the kind of people who today keep changing jobs, who invest in the lottery, who move to Las Vegas or Miami. The Missourians were not settled folks, not fully civilized, not church-goers and crop-planters, not storekeepers and wife-hoarders, though some of them owned slaves.

Soon there was trouble. Mobs assembled, dispersed, reassembled. October 1833, the thirty-first. Fawn M. Brodie: "Fifty men attacked an outlying Mormon colony west of the Big Blue River, unroofed and partially demolished ten cabins, whipped and stoned the men, and drove the women and children shrieking into the woods. When this was repeated on subsequent nights, the Mormons began to organize for defense."

The mobs grew. Both sides strengthened. In November, on the fourth, one Mormon and two gentiles were killed in a battle. Rumors spread, serious violence was at hand. The Mormons were badly outnumbered.

The lieutenant governor called out the militia, Lieutenant Governor Lilburn Boggs—a landholder, a slaveholder, a gentile. He called a meeting and addressed the Mormons. He asked them to give up their weapons and promised to disarm the gentiles. The Mormons complied. Like a herd of amiable musk oxen, they surrendered their weapons.

Lilburn Boggs did not keep his promise, did not make the gentiles give up their weapons. The night after the meeting, the gentile mob "systematically sacked every Mormon community, beat and whipped the men, and drove the women and children out like cattle. Before morning twelve hundred people had been herded forth in the teeth of a November gale. A few fled to Clay County, where they were received with sympathy; the majority huddled for days among the cottonwoods lining the Missouri River, hungry, weaponless, and leaderless, praying passionately for a miracle."

No miracle came. The Mormons moved in scattered groups and regathered. They went from Clay County to Caldwell County to Daviess County. They resettled in Daviess County, Missouri.

My Apartment

I needed to get organized, needed to get to work. In the Fred Myer store I found a shoe rack that looked like a small bookcase, the kind that would fit nicely on the top of my desk. I loaded it with stationery and bills and a stapler and my address book and my Mexican turtle and some stamps.

I opened my box of other Mexican curios and assembled a group of Day-of-the-Dead figures: several man skeletons dressed in suits and cowboy hats with bottles of beer in their hands and several lady skeletons in fancy dresses carrying handbags and wearing hats adorned with fake ostrich feathers. These characters are a warning: no matter how gleeful or fancy your life may be today, tomorrow you will be dead.

At the far left, sitting not on the shoe rack but on the desk proper, I placed the best of my treasures, another dead lady, made of modeled clay and about fourteen inches tall. Though her head was a skull, her neck a column of vertebrae, and her hands nothing but finger bones, the rest of her was horse-track elegance. Her full-length, long-sleeved, form-fitting gown was royal blue, with occasional white polka dots and random, vague, yellow splotches.

Day-of-the-Dead Woman

Her hat was huge, shaped approximately like the lid to a garbage can, adorned with two teal palm fronds and a cluster of gray hibiscus blossoms. She had a blotch of black hair clinging to each side of her skull, and in the hollows beside her mouth, where her cheeks once were, were stuck large blossoms, also teal.

At first glance her dress seemed to have a plunging neckline, but closer inspection revealed a mat of flesh-colored leaves surmounted by another small cluster of blossoms, purple, gray, and flesh-colored, all of which formed a kind of necklace. Also hanging around her neck was a long cord that supported a pair of horse-race binoculars, placed about at the point where her navel used to be. Her right arm was bent at the elbow, and from between the index and middle finger bones of that hand, which was held, palm-down, almost parallel to the surface of my desk and at the upper level of her right hip, a long cigarette protruded upward, surmounted by a glowing red tip. Both the cigarette and one of her fingers had broken off during my transit north from Mexico to Salt Lake City, but I had glued them back on.

My dead lady also had a snake draped around her neck. Its head and forked tongue rested on her right wrist, and its tail reached all the way down to her left finger bones, which were placed about where her left hip bone must have connected to her left thigh bone. The snake was teal, spotted with blue, and had an olive-green rattle at the end of his tail. He was not exactly smiling, but he did have a happy look upon his face. His eyes were wide with mischievous curiosity. He looked alive, as did the woman's breasts, her only sign of flesh, hidden beneath her dress. These features seemed related, the snake, the cigarette, and the breasts. A hint of original sin, a hint of the power of sex.

Two other curios adorned my shoe rack. At the far right was a small glass coffin containing a figure of Padre Kino, who had built a string of missions stretching from San Xavier, near Tucson, down to the southern end of the Mexican state of Sonora. What are thought to be Father Kino's actual bones are on display under glass in the town of Magdalena, where I bought my own version of his coffin and body. Like those of the lady's snake, Father Kino's eyes were wide open, but not mischievously so. He looked innocent, stunned, uneasy, nothing like how I imagined the real Father Kino—bold, adventurous, worldly, and strong.

Also in Magdalena I bought a statue of the Virgin, which I placed at the center of my shoe rack display, blessing all the other figures. Her gown and head covering were white, her belt was gold, her cape was blue and fringed with gold, her feet were bare, and she had a gold necklace about her neck. I could not discern any breasts, but she was definitely wearing makeup around her eyes and on her lips and cheeks, and her face was framed by luxuriant dark hair. She did not exude the same lustiness as the skeleton woman, but she was a definite proto-babe.

Daviess County

1838. Five years had passed since the last Mormon migration, the last Mormon retreat. Now they were living in Daviess County, Missouri, in and around the town of Gallatin, the county seat.

The gentiles had welcomed the Mormons, helped them out, lived with them in peace, accepted their ways. At first. Over time they grew tired of these strangers, these people who kept to themselves and prospered, who bought the best farmland and had so many wives. These people who seemed destined to take over the county, if not the state.

There had been one election, a bad election from the Mormon point of view. Lilburn Boggs, the lieutenant governor who had betrayed the Mormons in Independence, had been elected governor of the state of Missouri. Now it was the sixth of August, 1838, another election day. Thirty Mormons gathered to vote in Gallatin; one hundred gentiles were already there.

William Peniston, a candidate for local office, addressed the crowd, urging the gentiles to block the Mormons from voting: "They are a set of horse thieves, liars, and counterfeiters. They'll swear a false oath on any occasion to save another Mormon. They are thieves and knaves and dupes in the bargain, and no property is safe in Daviess County if they continue to pour into this area. If you suffer the Mormons to vote in this election, it will mean the end of your suffrage."

John Doyle Lee was there, lounging near a stack of oak hearts. Oak hearts "four feet long, and weighing about seven pounds." He heard the talk and saw what happened.

When the first Mormon went to vote, a gentile blocked his path, saying: "Daviess County don't allow Mormons to vote no more than niggers." Then the gentile hit the Mormon and knocked him down.

The Mormons were prepared for this reception. Their leader, John L. Butler, signaled them into action. They picked up the oak hearts and attacked, felling some gentiles as the others ran.

Butler addressed the remaining crowd. "This day I'm going to have my vote, and I'll die fighting before I'm driven from these polls without it." The Mormons went to the polls. The Mormons voted. The five years of peace was over.

Narrative as Meaning

You may be looking for a point. There isn't a point. Except to say that there isn't a point. All there is is narrative, narrative and being, the narrative of being, the narrative of human existence. The narrative can be amusing, even funny. The narrative can be sad, even tragic. But none of it has any meaning, because human existence has no point.

Mormonism is one of the narratives of human existence, funny and tragic and meaningless. That Mormonism thinks life has a point is one reason why it is funny. People who think human life has meaning are funny, in the absurdist, existentialist way of being funny.

That Mormonism thinks life has a point is one reason so much of Mormon history is tragic. People who think human life has a point are agents of tragedy, magnets for tragedy. This is a case of the One True Way being in conflict with all the wrong ways.

Eventually the conflict will lead to tragedy, and a lot of people will end up injured or dead.

Haun's Mill

The gentiles got knocked in the head and ran away. The Mormons stayed to vote and then went home.

The gentiles stopped running and regathered, really angry now. They took action: "Armed bands of Missourians prowled about, firing haystacks and granaries, stealing horses and cattle, and whipping Mormon farmers. Daily it became clearer…the gentiles were hell-bent to drive the Mormons out."

General Lucas was in charge of the militia. He wrote to Governor Boggs vowing that "those base and degraded beings will be exterminated from the face of the earth." Governor Boggs agreed and issued this order: "The Mormons must be treated as enemies and must be exterminated or driven from the state…. Their outrages are beyond all description." The Mormons had farmed successfully, had formed a cohesive and loving community, had prospered, had knocked a few heads and voted.

The Mormons were scattered throughout Daviess County. They were in Gallatin, in Far West, where Joseph had his headquarters, and they were in Haun's Mill, an outlying settlement, a small village.

On the thirtieth of October, 1838, the gentile militia marched into Haun's Mill. Fawn M. Brodie:

> The Mormons had fled into the blacksmith shop, which they thought would make an admirable fort, but it had proved instead to be a slaughterhouse. Great cracks yawned between the logs of the shop, and the Missourians, hiding behind trees, picked off the Mormons at their leisure as if they had been killing cattle in a pen. When the women fled toward the brush, the men shot at them in derision. Old Thomas McBride fell wounded and surrendered his gun, whereupon one of the mob coolly hacked him to pieces with a corn-cutter.

After shooting down every Mormon they could see, the mob entered the blacksmith shop to finish off the wounded. They found nine-year-old Sardis Smith hiding under the bellows. His younger brother, shot through the hip, and pretending to be dead, heard the men drag Sardis out from his hiding-place.

"Don't shoot," said one militiaman, "it's just a boy."

"It's best to hive them when we can. Nits will make lice," a man replied, and placing his rifle near the boy's head, blew out his brains.

Word came back to Far West, back to Joseph. Joseph saw the handwriting on the wall of Haun's Mill, that Governor Boggs had ordered the extermination of the Mormons. Joseph ordered two men to approach the Mormons' only gentile friend: "Find General Doniphan, and beg like a dog for peace."

Joseph was arrested. The other leaders were arrested. All the Mormons were ordered from the state. Their homes and lands were taken from them.

Knowing well that General Doniphan was friendly toward the Mormons, General Lucas ordered him to execute the Mormon leaders early the next morning.

At dawn the condemned were awakened and led to the square. General Doniphan addressed Joseph and the Mormon leaders: "By God, you have been sentenced by the court-martial to be shot this morning; but I will be damned if I will have…the disgrace of it. I have ordered my brigade to take up the line of march, and to leave the camp, for I consider it to be cold-blooded murder!"

When General Doniphan and his men marched out of town, General Lucas lost his nerve. He delayed his order. The Mormons were returned to jail.

When the Mormon leaders promised to lead their people out of Missouri, they were released. The Mormons gave up all they owned and moved across the Mississippi River into Illinois, searching again for Eden. They found their Zion. They founded the Mormon city, Nauvoo, Illinois.

The Meaning of Narrative

I was wrong when I said there is no point. No point to human
life. I was in a mood. Human life does have a point. The point is
love. Love one another. Love your neighbor. Love yourself. Love
your neighbor as you love yourself. Do unto your neighbor as you
do unto yourself. Do unto your neighbor as you would have your
neighbor do unto you.

How hard is this? Oh, it is hard. It is the hardest thing of all. But
do it. It is the point, the only point.

A Baseball Game

Sheila was living in her house with her three adopted daughters,
a cat, and a dog. Sean had moved out. I was living in my apartment.
Two months had gone by, maybe three. Sheila and I having lunch
every day. Spending some afternoon hours in the apartment or
taking long walks. Discussing when I would meet the girls.

They were seven, eight, and nine years old. Half sisters—one
mother, three anonymous fathers, one adoptive mother, one absent
adoptive father, one prospective looming stepfather. Crystal, the
middle daughter, had written me a letter. She wanted us to meet.

We decided on a baseball game. A Sunday afternoon in early
May 2000. We would gather outside the ballpark.

I arrived first, parked on the street and waited. As Sheila arrived
in her car, drove past me, and parked, three faces stared out the
back window, brown faces. Three sets of eyes so deeply brown they
were black stared out the back window at me.

Sheila introduced us. The older girls, Melanie and Crystal,
seemed matter-of-fact, almost blasé. The youngest girl, Rebekkah,
hid behind her mommy.

We walked a block to the corner. As we started to cross the street,
the oldest girl took my hand, did not let go until we were seated.
The middle girl chattered for most of the game. The youngest,
Rebekkah, held back for six innings, then crawled onto my lap,
where she stayed for the rest of the game.

Peter and Rebekkah at the Baseball Game

Part III
Deaths and Wrestling

Joseph in Nauvoo

The escape to Illinois saved the Mormons and brought them a few years of relative, diminishing peace, years of internal change. The battle with the outside world was in remission. The trouble inside the church was only starting. The Mormons built their town, established businesses, designed and constructed a temple, tilled the surrounding farmland.

The church was growing. Converts, true believers, people willing to suffer for their beliefs, continued to join the Mormons.

Joseph was changing, had changed. Moroni's prophet, Earth's sole wearer of the mantle of God, had become hardened through unending conflict with the world. Had become combative, defensive, increasingly convinced of the rightness of his thinking, of his righteousness, of his sense of divine inspiration, of his sense of divinity. Joseph had all the answers. Joseph was in charge, was not to be doubted or questioned, was acquainted with violence.

He had seen his people attacked and killed. He had seen his people fight back. He knew they would have to fight again. For the church to survive and conquer, they would have to fight as a matter of policy.

In 1838 Joseph had sanctioned the creation of a secret group called the "Sons of Dan," the "Danites." The Biblical prophet Daniel had likened the kingdom of God to a stone that rolled down a mountain, smashing everything secular in its path. In this way would Joseph's Danites deal with the gentiles. The gentile Christians had smashed the Mormon Christians. The Mormon Christians would be ready to smash the gentiles.

Two of Joseph's closest advisors, Sidney Rigdon and Samson Avard, were placed in command of the Danites. Though Joseph disguised his participation in the group, he recorded Avard's charge to his captains:

> Know ye not, brethren, that it will soon be your privilege to take your respective companies and go out on a scout on the borders of the settlements, and take to yourselves spoils of the goods of the ungodly Gentiles? for it is written, the riches of the Gentiles shall be consecrated to my people, the house of Israel; and thus you will waste away the Gentiles by robbing and plundering them of their property; and in this way we will build up the kingdom of God, and roll forth the little stone that Daniel saw cut out of the mountain without hands, and roll forth until it filled the whole earth. For this is the very way that God destines to build up His kingdom in the last days. If any of us should be recognized, who can harm us? for we will stand by each other and defend one another in all things.... I would swear a lie to clear any of you; and if this would not do, I would put them or him under the sand.... And if one of this Danite society reveals any of these things, I will put him where the dogs *cannot bite him.*

Against the outside world in Missouri, the Danites had operated in the dark, in the shadows, as a guerrilla force. Against their internal enemies in Nauvoo, in Illinois, they operated in the back alleys, on the river, in the fields and the woods, as Joseph's secret police.

Playing Wrestle

Monday. A cold Monday in May 2002. I was outside wrestling. Now I am back inside, sitting at my desk, trying to find some vague connection between the Mormons and the family.

Crystal and Rebekkah are still outside. They went out after

dinner, outside to wrestle. It is cold outside, cold for May, fifty-three degrees. The wind is blowing hard. The wind is always blowing at the Pond House. Once it came in a window and blew the TV set off a table. Or so I was told by the previous owner.

The girls said they were going outside to play wrestle. A month after we met, I saw them wrestle, two years ago, May 2000. They weren't playing wrestle, they were trying to kill each other. Seven years old and eight.

This happened in the backyard of their house in Utah, in the sandbox. I was in the kitchen and saw them out the window. I went out to make peace, to be their mediator.

Salt Lake City is the capital of the Kingdom of Moroni, the Zion of the Mormons, their Edenic paradise. The girls are not Mormons. Maybe they are gentiles. Their birth mother was Jewish. They are adopted. There is a lot about their heritage we do not know. For sure they are not Mormons.

But they are sisters, half sisters. Three girls with one birth mother, three birth fathers, one adoptive mother, one adoptive father, one latter-day stepfather. Each of them has two sisters—I mean half sisters.

These two were trying to kill each other, out there in the sand box in Salt Lake City two years ago. Sometimes sisters try to kill each other. Sometimes brothers try to kill each other. Saints? Do saints try to kill each other?

Sometimes Mormon saints have tried to kill each other. Sometimes Mormons have killed Mormons. Sometimes saints have killed saints.

Joseph and the Doctrine of Blood Atonement

Mostly it was a Brigham thing, the practice of blood atonement. Evidence comes down from the days of Joseph, but mostly it was a Brigham thing. Blood atonement—spilling blood for the remission of sin. Other people's blood, other people's sins, the blood and sins of the backsliding brethren. Spilling their blood for the remission of their sins. Righteous murder, retribution—for apostasy, for faithlessness, for the absence of loyalty, the absence of blind loyalty. For dissension, for questioning the ways of the prophet, the prophet Joseph, the prophet Brigham.

References to blood atonement are few in the histories of Mormons and Mormonism. In *Utah: The Right Place*, his "official centennial history," Thomas G. Alexander says only that, in 1887, "the church leadership disavowed blood atonement as an authentic Mormon doctrine." No definition of the term, no examples of the practice, nothing but this. The true history comes from the people who were there.

John Doyle Lee, the Mormon scapegoat, kept a diary, from the time of his conversion in 1838 to the time of his execution in 1877. More than occasionally in those pages, he mentions instances of blood atonement. In his autobiography, the jail cell *Confessions* he wrote while awaiting his execution, he summarized its history:

> I knew of many men being killed in Nauvoo.... It was then the rule that all the enemies of Joseph Smith should be killed, and I know of many a man who was quietly put out of the way by the orders of Joseph and his Apostles while the Church was there.
>
> It has always been a well understood doctrine of the Church that it was right and praiseworthy to kill every person who spoke evil of the prophet.... The doctrine is still believed, and no year passes without one or more of those who have spoken evil of Brigham Young being killed, in a secret manner.

The Danites were the atoners, the agents of atonement, the killers, Joseph's mob, his cadre of hit men. Samson Avard, co-leader of the Danites, bragged: "When I meet one damning and cursing the presidency...I will get a bowl of brandy and get him half-drunk. Then, taking him by the arm into the woods or brush, I will be into his guts in a minute and put him under the sod." To which Sidney Rigdon supplied the refrain: "All the burial he shall have will be in

Avenging Angel, Orrin Porter Rockwell

a turkey buzzard's guts."

By the time of Nauvoo, Orrin Porter Rockwell had become the most active of the Danites. Orrin Porter Rockwell, the most efficient killer in the history of Mormonism. The one-man precursor to the Mafia's Murder Incorporated. Joseph's body guard, his avenging angel.

The Family Neighborhood

I moved into the house early in July, in the year 2000, into Sheila's house on the near southeast side of Salt Lake City. One block east of Liberty Park, where we went for walks, to play Frisbee, to ride on the merry-go-round. From whence, on the twenty-fourth of July in the year 2000, we watched the parade commemorating the one-hundred-fifty-third anniversary of Pioneer Day. The day in 1847 when the Mormons had arrived in the Kingdom of Moroni.

We would take evening walks, the five of us. Me, fifty-nine years old, Sheila, thirty-six, Melanie, eight, Crystal, seven, Rebekkah, six. Downhill to Liberty Park on the west or uphill to the east, toward the foothills of the Wasatch Range. We discovered a Mormon enclave, a ward or stake house, a meeting place and place where weddings were performed, baptisms. A place set in a parklike enclosure, fenced, a creek running through it, a place with benches where we would sit, Sheila and I, watching the girls investigate the creek.

Two avenues paralleled that creek as it tumbled downhill through a wilderness of trees, above the Mormon ward or stake house. One avenue was called Yale—the one on the left hand looking east. The right-hand avenue was called Harvard. We would walk up one and down the other. We would admire the houses on Yale Avenue, the houses that backed up to the creek. We would admire the wilderness on the creek side of Harvard Avenue.

We would talk and become acquainted. We would joke with one another and say, "Look both ways before crossing the street." We would stop the ice cream truck and buy treats.

The Shooting of Governor Boggs

In May of 1842 Governor Boggs of Missouri was shot three times in the head by an unknown assailant. Lilburn Boggs, the man who, as lieutenant governor, had betrayed the Mormons into the hands of the militia by seducing them to relinquish their arms. The man who, as governor five years later, had ordered that the Mormons "be exterminated or driven from the state."

A year before the shooting, in 1841, Joseph had prophesied the death of Boggs. According to rumor, he had also promised a reward of five hundred dollars to anyone who would cleanse the earth of this man. Two days after word of the shooting arrived in Nauvoo, Orrin Porter Rockwell, Joseph's avenging angel, arrived in Nauvoo, driving a fine new carriage and team, and bragging that he had been in Missouri.

Though badly wounded, Boggs survived. Hearing the rumors, he ordered that Rockwell be arrested and charged with the shooting. Evidence was sparse. Not flimsy, sparse. Rockwell had a compelling motive. He was in Missouri at the time of the shooting. He could offer no convincing reason for being there. He was the only suspect. But no one could place him at the scene. No one had seen him pull the trigger. To everyone's surprise, he was acquitted.

Later a posse from Missouri arrived in Nauvoo to arrest Joseph on the same charge. Joseph avoided extradition by hiding out and through legal maneuvering. The outside world was closing in.

Shrimp Poop in the Lake

Sometimes we would visit the lake. Drive through the nature preserves or walk on the beaches, the strange, deserted, mud or sharp-pebble encrusted beaches of the Great Salt Lake. Salt Lake City occupies the edge of the desert, at the eastern edge of the Great Basin, at the western edge of the Wasatch Range of the Rocky Mountains. Snow and rain fall on the mountains, and water flows down the slopes and into the lake, the lake with no outlet, the lake from which no water can flow. Gradually the fresh water evaporates in the heat. The water that remains becomes increasingly saturated with various minerals, among them a prodigious amount of salt.

So toxic is the water in the Great Salt Lake that almost nothing can live in it. Sea gulls occasionally visit, but the only true survivor is the brine shrimp, tasty to the gulls but to no one else. The brine shrimp are the source of the small, sharp, rocklike objects called oolites that cover the beaches and the bottom of the Great Salt Lake. At the center of each oolite is a pearl of brine shrimp poop. The minerals suspended in the water are drawn to the poop by some kind of electrolysis. The minerals stick and solidify, and the resultant objects become oolites.

The Death of an Old Lady

A gossipy old woman lived in Nauvoo. A gossipy old woman died in Nauvoo, in the river, the Mississippi River. She had figured something out. She had caught on to the secret called polygamy.

I found the story in a footnote in Harold Schindler's biography of Orrin Porter Rockwell: "If rumors bruited about Nauvoo were true, Orrin Porter Rockwell...and Joseph Smith had drowned an elderly Mormon woman who gossiped openly about the prophet's private life and was embarrassing high officials of the church with her disclosures."

Late one night in Nauvoo there was a commotion. A commotion outside the hotel in Nauvoo, the Mormon hotel called the Nauvoo House. A few people were in the lobby, Mormons and visitors, only a few. One of them told this story.

First there was a commotion, an argument. Then an old lady was led away by two men. Then there was silence, a quiet half hour in Nauvoo. Then there were Joseph and Orrin, stumbling back into the hotel, later that night, soaking wet.

The body of the gossipy old woman was found the next morning, lying on the bank of the Mississippi River.

The story may be apocryphal, semi-apocryphal. Still, the woman did drown; Orrin Porter Rockwell was a killer; Joseph sanctioned

Disposing of a Body

killing; the two of them were there that night; two men argued with the woman and led her off; Joseph and Orrin returned to the hotel soaking wet; the woman's body was found the next day, soaking wet in the river.

This happened late in the life of Joseph. During the years of Joseph's arrogance and his pride.

Red Butte Creek

Sometimes rain or snow will fall in the desert and find its way into the Great Salt Lake. The rest of the source water comes from the creeks that run down the western slope of the mountains. Seven of these creeks flow through the metropolitan area of Salt Lake City. Within a day of their arrival, the first Mormon settlers had dammed City Creek, created a crude system of irrigation, and sown some seeds.

Irrigation turned that edge of the desert green. The early Mormons were inveterate planters, of trees in addition to crops, grains, and grasses. Salt Lake City today is a green and leafy place, thanks to their efforts and to the system of irrigation they established.

The system is still there, though little used today. I learned of its existence one Tuesday evening when I arrived at the house about an hour after a severe thunderstorm had passed. What looked like a river was rushing down the dead-ending side street, Princeton Avenue, across 800 East Street, and directly onto the driveway, and into the basement, of the house standing there. A couple of men were tending a diversion dam of plywood and cinder blocks.

This made me wonder about the creek we had found on the property of the ward or stake house, the creek that had to run through our neighborhood somewhere. On a map I found its name, Red Butte Creek, next creek south of City Creek. The other five, from north to south, are Emigration, Parley's (named after the pioneer and Mormon divine, Parley Pratt), Mill, Big Cottonwood, and Little Cottonwood.

The northern four flow through the city proper, and each is diverted underground for a good bit of its transit. The southern three flow on the surface through such contiguous municipalities as South Salt Lake, Holladay, Murray, and Sandy. All seven creeks flow into a sluggish ditch known grandly as the Jordan River. The Jordan River in turn flows into the Great Salt Lake. Nothing flows out of the Great Salt Lake.

At the time of the deluge, I knew only that Red Butte Creek flowed underground through that neighborhood. Using my map, I set out to find it. The early part was easy: the creek emerges from Red Butte Canyon just above the University of Utah, runs through Fort Douglas and past some athletic fields, then into Sunnyside Park, then into Miller Park. At the end of Miller Park, the creek goes briefly underground before reemerging on private property and running down the hill between Yale and Harvard Avenues. When the land begins to flatten, the creek emerges onto the grounds of the ward or stake house.

After that it goes underground almost permanently—it reappears briefly just west of 900 East Street—but somewhere between 1100 East Street and 900 East Street, perhaps on McClelland Street near its intersection with either Princeton, Harvard, or Yale Avenue, I found a locked system of valves whereby the underground stream could be diverted into a surface irrigation system that sends water down small canals running along the alleys. The immense volume of water produced by that thunderstorm had defeated the system, causing most of the water to flow onto the city streets. Thus had Red Butte Creek come to flood that house on 800 East Street.

Polygamy

On the twelfth of August, 1843, Joseph informed the High Council of his revelation on polygamy. He had studied the lifestyles of the early prophets in the Bible and had noticed that they had wives. Not a wife but wives. All the wives they wanted. Joseph was himself a prophet, and he hungered for wives. He checked with God. God said, "OK." God said, "That's the way I planned it." Maybe God said, "I didn't say no wives. I said mo' wives."

The council was ordered to keep the revelation a secret. All of the apostles were free to take wives, but the people must not know. When the people noticed the clusters of women living in the homes of the apostles, rumors began to spread. Most of the people were uncomfortable with what they heard. Many were angry. Still, Joseph and his cronies took more wives. In the last years of his life, Joseph took forty-eight new wives.

Joseph's ego swelled as Nauvoo grew. As the city became larger, more powerful, and grandiose, Joseph's ego became larger, more powerful, and grandiose. He went public with polygamy. He formed a militia, a Mormon militia, four thousand men strong. He declared himself commander. He wore a fancy uniform. He carried a large sword. He rode upon a white stallion. Joseph rode around on his stallion wearing his uniform and waving his phallic sword. He declared himself a candidate for the presidency of the United States of America.

The Battle in the Backyard

I was in the kitchen doing something. Sheila was in her office at the medical center, at the University of Utah, helping doctors write readable prose. Melanie was God knows where, maybe in her room looking at a book. Crystal and Rebekkah were in the backyard, playing in the sandbox.

I looked out the window and saw that they were fighting. They were trying to kill each other. I ran outside, got between them, pushed them apart. I explained that sisters should love one another. They listened reluctantly. After a space of time and a lot of my preaching, they agreed with me and shook hands.

Then Crystal picked up a truck and tried to brain Rebekkah. I got my arm between the truck and the head just in time. Rebekkah hit the dirt, scrabbled forth, sank her teeth into Crystal's calf. Crystal lifted the truck.

I practiced the gentle art of mediation. I sat on Rebekkah. I pinned Crystal's arms so she couldn't move. I preached sisterly love. I held on until no one was struggling. I made them go to their rooms. I sighed.

I went to the kitchen. I poured myself a glass of lemonade. Before I could sit down, I heard furniture breaking, bodies hitting the floor. I ran back upstairs.

William Law

Joseph was already president of Nauvoo. He was in charge of everything that happened in Nauvoo. He oversaw all the business that was conducted and decided who could be part of the action, and how. William Law was a Mormon businessman, an apostle in the Mormon church, a leading citizen, a close friend to Joseph Smith. But he was troubled. Troubled by Joseph's egomania, his control of business, his doctrine of polygamy.

William Law had a wife named Jane. Joseph Smith cast eyes upon Jane. He looked at her with spiritual sight and saw that she was comely. When he asked her to be his wife, Jane said she was already married, married to William Law. Then she went home and told her husband.

William Law became angry. No, he had already been angry. Now he was really angry.

According to Wallace Stegner, William "had long known about the revelation on spiritual marriage and about the secret plural wives, and had kept silence, hoping that Joseph would come to his senses. Instead, he had come to Jane."

William bought a printing press and started a newspaper. He called his paper the *Nauvoo Expositor*, and he used its one issue to expose Joseph.

Joseph had the type scattered and the press destroyed. He ordered that the press building be burned to the ground. Things were going bad in the city of Nauvoo, in the tight community of Mormons.

Miss Janelle's Theory of the Sexes

The morning after the battle in the sandbox, I drove the girls to day care. All three of them were buckled in the back seat, and two of them were simmering. Then Crystal pushed Rebekkah. Rebekkah stomped on Crystal's foot. Crystal dug her elbow into Rebekkah's ribs. I preached sisterly love. Melanie crawled over Rebekkah and got between the warriors in the back seat.

I talked to Miss Janelle, the director of day care. I told Miss Janelle what had happened in the car. I was still upset, from the car and from the sandbox. Miss Janelle laughed. I wanted to seem knowledgeable and cool, so I chuckled uneasily.

I told Miss Janelle that I had raised boys before. I told her this was different. Miss Janelle explained things to me. She said that boys will fight and then it is over.

"But it is never over with girls," Miss Janelle said. "Girls seethe."

Now it is 2002. May. They were play wrestling, Crystal and Rebekkah, the same two warriors. They were playing a game called *wrestle*. I played with them. We rolled around on the grass. The dog barked and barked. Crystal jumped on my stomach. Rebekkah pretended to beat me with a branch.

Crystal chased Rebekkah. Rebekkah got on her bike. "You messed with the wrong girl this time," Rebekkah said. She pretended she was going to run Crystal down with her bike. Both of them were laughing.

The girls were all right. They were just having fun. I went inside, came up here to my office to work on the connections, the connections between the family life and the Mormon life.

Things were coming to a head in Nauvoo. William Law and Joseph were both seething. The people were uncomfortable with what was going on, the people inside the church and the people outside. The citizens of Illinois had about had it with the Mormons.

The Last Days of Joseph

Five years to bring Illinois, once markedly friendly, to a hostility as savage as that of Missouri ever was, and to start the whole state, from high-placed politicians to the lowest border ruffian, crying that the Mormons must go.

—Wallace Stegner

1844. Other things had changed since the Mormons were welcomed to Illinois. Nauvoo had grown from barely a settlement to a town of twenty thousand. The largest town in Illinois, a town like a beehive, active and prosperous enough to terrify the locals.

The citizens of Illinois were no longer sympathetic to the Mormon settlement. Fawn M. Brodie: "To them the Nauvoo theocracy was a malignant tyranny that was spreading as swiftly and dangerously as a Mississippi flood and that might eventually engulf the very government of the United States." Joseph had become the Grand Lieutenant Colonel Poobah Prophet of Nauvoo. Now he wanted to be the Grand Lieutenant Colonel Poobah Prophet of America, the president.

The editor of the *Warsaw Signal* sounded a call to arms: "War and extermination is inevitable! CITIZENS ARISE, ONE AND ALL!!! Can you *stand* by and suffer such INFERNAL DEVILS! to ROB men of their property and Rights, without avenging them? We have no time for comments; every man will make his own. LET it be made with POWDER AND BALLS!!!"

The gentiles of Illinois began gathering in mobs. Joseph had had it with the gentiles and with the mobs: "Here is wishing," he said, "that all of the mobocrats of the nineteenth century were in the middle of the sea, in a stone canoe, with an iron paddle, that a shark might swallow the canoe, and the shark be thrust into the nethermost part of hell, and the door locked, the key lost, and a blind man hunting for it." Joseph had a way with words. Joseph wrote The Book of Mormon.

Governor Ford of the great state of Illinois had had enough. He ordered Joseph and his inner circle to "submit immediately to the Carthage constable and come to that city for trial."

Joseph saw that the end was near. With a few of his closest advisors, he escaped across the Mississippi River in a leaky rowboat in the middle of the night. Then he decided he should not desert his people. On June 24 he returned to Nauvoo, was arrested, was taken to the Carthage jail.

A trial was planned. The Illinois militia did not want a trial: "Clear the way and let us see old Joe, the prophet of God.... We'll use him up and kill all the damned Mormons!"

Governor Ford said no to vigilantism. He said there must be a trial. He traveled to Carthage to preserve the peace by his presence. Joseph was certain that the mob would kill him and begged the governor to get him away from Carthage. Governor Ford promised to do just that.

Then the governor came up with another plan. He would dismiss the militia. The mob would go away, things would quiet down, and he could leave town. Joseph and the other Mormon leaders would stay in the Carthage jail until their trial.

The militia had its own plan: "Our troops will be discharged this morning in obedience to orders, and for a sham we will leave the town; but...we will return and kill those men, if we have to tear the jail down."

The militia was discharged, the mob left town, the governor left town, the militia returned and stormed the jail.

Hyrum Smith was killed immediately, Joseph's brother Hyrum. John Taylor was shot five times. Willard Richards was shot in the ear. Joseph emptied his gun, all six bullets. One of them shattered a man's arm.

Men rushed into the cell. When Joseph sprang to the window, a bullet caught him from behind. He fell from the window to the ground.

Four men took aim and shot Joseph at point blank range. As the prophet lay dying a man rushed forward to cut off his head.

Just then the sun broke through thick clouds and shone upon Joseph. The militia were stunned at this sign from above, and they ran.

Joseph died alone on the street in front of the Carthage jail, bathed in an ironic ray of sun.

Part IV
Migrations and Settlings

The Last Days of Nauvoo

Nauvoo lasted a year and a half, after the death of Joseph. The gentile militias would have attacked, but the Mormon Legion of Danites was too strong. Converts kept arriving, from the eastern states, from England and Wales. The population of Nauvoo grew to twenty-five thousand.

The temple was under construction and had to be finished. The recent converts needed to have their endowments bestowed upon them, their endowments from God, endowments that could be bestowed only in a temple, a Mormon temple built by Mormon hands. The people knew they had to leave. They wanted to go. But first the temple, first the endowments, first the blessing of the journey.

The endowments, the fundamental step for full sainthood: the washing of feet, the baptism, the anointment by oil or water, and the instruction in rights, duties, and obligations.

The prophet was dead. Long live the prophet. Candidates stepped forth and meetings were held. Sidney Rigdon, James Jesse Strang, and many others wanted the job. But when Brigham Young stood to speak, a miracle occurred. Pudgy, short, and plain, he seemed to grow lean, tall, and handsome, like Joseph. And when he opened his mouth, he spoke in Joseph's voice. He spoke the words of God through Joseph's voice. The people listened, astonished. The other candidates stepped aside.

The Mormons were surrounded, hated by the gentiles, under a kind of siege. Then in September of 1845, Orrin Porter Rockwell was pursued while returning to town from Carthage. He turned in his saddle and shot one man dead. The governor—the hated Governor Ford—told the Mormons that it was time to go. On September 24 the Mormon leaders promised that the saints would be gone "as soon as the grass grows and water runs." They would leave Nauvoo. They would finish building their temple, use it once for the endowments, and leave it behind.

Spring 1846. The Mormons sold their houses and their land. They loaded their goods into wagons and left Illinois. They crossed over the Mississippi River, over the Iowa Territory, what would be the state of Iowa, crossed over the Missouri River, crossed into what would be Nebraska, regathered at Winter Quarters. At a settlement they founded and named Winter Quarters. North of Omaha, in what would someday be Nebraska. They stayed for the winter, preparing.

Spring 1847. The Mormons headed farther west, toward Zion. They had identified Zion. Zion was out west, on the western slope of the Rocky Mountains, at the edge of the desert. A terrible place. By reputation a hideous place. A place of no rain. A place of saltwater. A place where no one could live. Where no one sane would live. A place where the Mormons could live alone. A place without gentiles. A place without mobs. A place without gentile mobs.

The great migration took place in 1847. The first group of Mormons traveled on foot and by ox cart across America, from eastern Nebraska to what would be western Utah, in 1847. The Mormons began settling the valley of the Great Salt Lake in 1847. They arrived in July, on July 24, on Pioneer Day.

Purchase of the Pond House

In May or June I returned alone to Gettysburg to look for a house. Sometime in May or June, in the year 2000. Neal, my real estate agent, had searched the listings. The first day we looked at eight or ten houses, all over the county. Neal saved the best one for last, the one he thought we should have. A suburban house, relatively new, a tight and tidy house on a tight and tidy street. No trees but many nice lawns.

"Fewer problems with a new house," Neal said. "Plumbing, heating, wiring, insulation, all in good shape and right up to code. New kitchen and bathrooms, up-to-date fixtures. You can't go wrong buying a house like this. This house has you written all over it."

I wanted to be in the country. I wanted an old house. I wanted woods and a pond.

We started early the next day, looked at a bunch of houses, stopped for lunch at Tommy's Pizza. "OK," said Neal. "I found one more. When I did the original search, I specified two full baths, one for the adults and one for the children. Last night I ran the search again, this time specifying one full bath and one half bath. I found an old farm house in the country. We might as well take a look."

"Might as well," I replied.

The house was located seven miles west of town, almost to the foothills of the Appalachians. It was built before the Civil War, in 1850, and had thirteen rooms total, four or five bedrooms; four nonworking fireplaces, three places where stoves had once been, a full attic, a paved basement, wiring, plumbing, a furnace for heat, one full bath, one half bath.

Way at the back end of the L-shaped extension, on the second floor, we also found a small, neglected room with an old bathtub, a radiator, a homemade cabinet on the wall, a hole in the floor where a toilet had once been. What could be a second full bath.

Outside, seven and a half acres, a woodlot, a pond, a meadow, a little creek. I looked at Neal. "How much are they asking?"

"This Is the Place"

And abruptly there it was, the whole great valley shimmering in summer heat, one of the great views of the continent. From where they stood above the alluvial fan of Emigration Creek, the Wasatch ran in an abrupt wall southward, but on the north it swung an arm around to

Brigham Young

half enclose the valley. Beginning nearly straight west of them, perhaps
twenty-five airline miles away, the high smooth crestline of the Oquirrhs
also ran southward until it all but met the Wasatch at a low notch on the
southern sky. And northward and westward from the northernmost foot
of the Oquirrhs, fabulous, dark blue, floating its pale islands, lapping
the world's rim, went the Great Salt Lake.

—Wallace Stegner

Brigham Young migrated across America in Wilford Woodruff's wagon, the first in line. Late in the trip Brigham came down with mountain fever, an illness that killed many, but by the end he was well again. Coming down the western face of the Wasatch Range, the party followed the narrow bed of Emigration Creek, crossing and recrossing the water and picking their way among the trees and rocks. Eventually the foliage thinned and the valley appeared.

According to Mormon legend, when Brigham stepped out of the wagon and looked at the view, he said, "This is the place."

Many years later a monument was erected, a state park established, to commemorate the moment. The park is called "This Is the Place" State Park. It sits on a bluff above Emigration Creek, in Salt Lake City, out near the University of Utah.

I lived in Salt Lake City, lived there for six months, in 2000, from March through August. I learned about the mountains. I learned about the Wasatch Range and became acquainted with the Oquirrhs, one of those isolated desert mountain ranges. I learned that Wasatch is pronounced WAH-*satch*. I learned that Oquirrhs is pronounced OAK-*ras*, like the strange greasy vegetable grown and eaten in the muddy lowlands of Alabama, Mississippi, and Georgia.

An Act of Sweet Idiocy

They had a cat, Sheila and the girls, a cat named Delores. Sometime in June, before I moved in, the cat had disappeared for a number of days. About a week after her reappearance, Delores began to grow. Her belly got bigger and bigger. Toward the end of the month, she had six kittens, enough for a basketball team with one sub. The girls were present at the birthing. Every time they thought it was over, another kitten would appear.

At the beginning of July, I moved in with them, with Sheila, the girls, the cat, and the kittens. Then came August, time to move the new family to Pennsylvania, to the Pond House, the house with the home office in which I am at this moment writing about the house. The closing on the house was scheduled for the twenty-first.

I rented a truck. I was to drive the truck to Pennsylvania. Melanie was to ride with me. The others were to follow later by air. I rented a trailer to carry my car. Later Sean, the other daddy, would move to Pennsylvania. He would drive the other car.

We loaded everything into the truck, everything of Sheila's we deemed worth moving. We talked about the cat, the mother cat and her kittens. The girls said they had to go with us to Pennsylvania. They were part of the family.

"How are we going to do this?" I asked. "Air mail? Federal Express?"

"No," said the girls. "You will take them in the truck."

"Are you crazy?" I replied. "I can't drive a truck two thousand miles with a cat and six kittens mewling and puking and crawling around. A big truck with furniture and junk and a car trailing along."

Sheila observed this discussion with teary eyes. "Melanie could watch the kittens while you drive," she said.

"Grrr," I replied. "We will need a dish for water and a dish for food and a litter box."

"Yay!" said the girls.

"You're so sweet," said Sheila.

"No," I said. "I'm not sweet. I'm just an idiot. Maybe a sweet idiot, but an idiot nevertheless."

He Never Said It

The moment was grand. The moment came after incredible hardship. Hardship in New York and Ohio and Missouri and Illinois and on the trip out.

The Mormons had been traveling for months, all summer long; across the great plains, across many rivers; over parched land, over the Rocky Mountains. Many Mormons had died along the way, many had been buried. Nearly everyone had been sick, including the prophet. Brigham Young had almost died from mountain fever.

Now they had arrived at their goal, and the time was right for a grand utterance. Brigham Young should have looked at the valley, the sacred site of refuge, the soon-to-be Kingdom of Moroni; he should have spread his arms in an encompassing gesture; he should have said, "This is the place." But he did not. Maybe he turned instead to Wilford Woodruff, clasped him by the shoulder, and said, "Wilford, are we done crossing that damn creek?"

In his journal, written at the time, Woodruff said that when Brigham saw the valley, he "expressed his full satisfaction in the appearance of the valley as a resting-place for the Saints, and was amply rewarded for his journey." That sounds a lot like Brigham. In his own journal entry for that day, Brigham mentioned that they had crossed the creek eighteen times and arrived at the camp at two in the afternoon. That sounds like him too.

The grand phrase itself seems to have been created thirty-three years later, on Pioneer Day, by an overexcited orator possessed by the spirit of the Angel Moroni.

Reverse Migration

We hit the road, all nine of us: Melanie and me and the cat and the six kittens. The car was on a trailer following along behind. Reverse migration across the breadth of America, following in reverse the route followed by the Mormons, from Utah through Nebraska, then on to Pennsylvania. Melanie and me and the truck and the car and the furniture and the junk and the cat Delores and the six kittens—Max, Polkadot, Duncan, Blackie, Happy, and Monkey. And a litter box, a bowl for food, a bowl for water.

When we stopped in the evening, we would replenish the food and water and clean the litter box. Before we drove off in the morning, we would do it again.

Melanie did her best to keep the kittens from causing an accident or getting lost or killed. Behind our seats near the floor was an opening to the back of the truck. Kittens would disappear in there for hours, prowling among the boxes and the chairs.

Melanie lounged in the shotgun seat, bare feet propped atop the dashboard, doing puzzles, listening to tunes, using her camera, reading me stories from her book. Sometimes the kittens would crawl up to her lap, then up her legs to the top of the dashboard, a vast, sloping plane that extended from just behind the steering wheel to the bottom of the windshield. The kittens would chase one another from side to side, tumbling, wrestling, playing before my eyes as we crossed Wyoming, Nebraska, Iowa, Illinois, Indiana, Ohio, and Pennsylvania. I concentrated on the road. The kittens did not cause an accident.

We stayed in cheap motels and ate in cafes. One night we went crazy and had steak. Sheila, Crystal, and Rebekkah flew in an airplane some days later, I don't remember how many.

We picked them up at the airport in Baltimore. We closed on the Pond House. We enrolled the girls in school, second grade, third grade, and fourth. We gathered the remnants of life, the remnants of many lives. We started to build the family, the new family: the cat, the six kittens, the three little girls and the adoptive mother and the new stepdad. The Whole Dern (as it later came to be known) Walker Clan, alive and well in the Pond House at last.

The Lost Tribes of Israel

Fleeing to western Utah, the Mormons had left their enemies, their gentile neighbors, behind. Now their neighbors were Indians, American Indians—in Mormon mythology, the last remnants of the Lost Ten Tribes of Israel. The tribes that had sailed to America to escape the destruction of Jerusalem in 600 BC. Thus spake Joseph in The Book of Mormon. Believe it if you can.

Nephi, son of Lehi, the leader of this band of immigrants, was opposed by Laman and Lemuel, his evil brothers. So evil was Laman that God placed a curse upon him and all his red-skinned descendants. God did not mention how the descendants would become red skinned. They just would.

The battles between the Nephites and the Lamanites continued for a thousand years before the Lamanites prevailed over their fair-skinned enemies. Thus the redskins, the American Indians, were the Hebrew remnants of the lost tribes of Israel, and ripe for conversion.

Unlike other western settlers, the Mormons approached the Indians with sympathy. They established missions designed to save the Indians rather than displace and slaughter them, as seemed to be the goal of the government agencies. Conflict was still inevitable, cultural conflict and conflict over land and animals. But the Mormon attitude was mostly friendly, and they tried to work things out, bless their pure polygamous hearts.

Meanwhile the western expansion continued. The movement westward of the whiteskins, the gentiles, the enemies of the Mormons. Even as early as this, the Mormons could hear sounds of feet marching from the East.

First Kitten Death at the Pond House

We closed on the house on the twenty-first of August, in the year 2000, the Pond House. We unloaded the truck, distributed the furniture among the thirteen rooms. Two or three rooms of furniture spread out over thirteen rooms. All my stuff was still at my old house, still to be divided with Jean. At least we had enough beds.

I started back to work right away. The girls started school on the twenty-sixth or twenty-seventh. Melanie rode one bus to Lincoln Elementary in Gettysburg, to her fourth-grade class. Crystal and Rebekkah rode another bus to Franklin Township Elementary in Cashtown, to second grade and third. Rebekkah was in second and Crystal was in third.

Sheila stayed home with the cats, applying for freelance jobs, copyediting and proofreading by mail, the sort of work she had done in an office in Salt Lake City.

Over the first weekend we bought a refrigerator, from Mr. Tipton, who sells used appliances in Hanover, Pennsylvania, about twelve miles away. My friend Wayne lent me a truck, Mr. Tipton lent me a dolly. I moved the refrigerator myself in Wayne's truck, using Mr. Tipton's dolly.

Mr. Tipton was coming on Monday to pick up his dolly. I left it inside the front door and went to work. I left early, even before the school buses had come. Sheila and the girls were standing by the front door, waiting for the buses. The kittens were there too, scampering and playing on the floor. One of them, Max, the curious one, mostly black with some white, took an interest in the dolly. He dug his claws into the straps and started climbing to the top.

The dolly fell over on him, unbalanced by his weight. The dolly was heavy, and Max was crushed by the dolly. Blood came gushing out of his mouth. Sheila and the girls screamed and cried, and Sheila called me on the phone.

"Jesus," I said to myself, set aside my work, grabbed my keys, and headed home. By the time I got there, Max was dead. I put his body into a plastic bag and carried it out to the garage. I hugged the girls, dried their tears, dropped them off at school. After dark that night I buried Max in the woods, in the wetlands, below the dam of the pond.

The Walker War

1847, the Mormons arrived in Utah. 1848, the Treaty of Guadelupe Hidalgo was signed, ending the Mexican War. The treaty placed most of the American Southwest under the control of the United States government. The Mormons already had a system of government in place, a very different system, a theocracy with Brigham Young at its head. Sprigs of conflict were already sprouting.

On the ninth of September, 1850, Washington took over governance of Utah (including what would be Nevada) by giving it territorial status. The Mormons were afraid that they would lose their kingdom, afraid that a gentile would be appointed governor, with absolute power of veto.

When President Fillmore appointed Brigham to be governor, that was good news. When he appointed three eastern gentiles to be federal judges, that was bad news. The judges could overturn Mormon law, could impose federal law, could try Mormons without Brigham's consent. The Mormons hated the outsiders, hated and feared them. A kind of civil war could break out, the judges at war with Governor Brigham, the United States at war with the Mormon people of Utah. It would be called the Utah War.

But first the Walker War.

1853, the seventeenth of July. A Mormon named James Ivie killed a Ute Indian in a trading dispute, a Ute named Shower-O-Cats, relative of Chief Walkara, known to the Mormons as Walker. Shower-O-Cats, what might have been my name driving that truck. When the Utes demanded a white man's death to even the score, the Mormons refused. The Indians went on a rampage, killed a Mormon guard, marched up Payson Valley. The pursuing Mormon militia killed six Utes.

The Mormons withdrew to their cities and forts, but the troubles continued into August and September. Two Mormons were killed in Park City. The Indians stole unprotected Mormon cattle and horses and killed Mormons found in isolated places. On the second of October, a group of nonwarring Utes arrived at the fort in Nephi and begged for protection. The paranoid Mormons slaughtered them all. At about that same time, a lone Pavhant Indian was killed, perhaps by a passing wagon train.

On 26 October 1853, just after these two events, Captain John W. Gunnison of the US Corps of Topographical Engineers and his seven men were massacred at their camp on the lower Sevier River in Pavhant territory. Perhaps the killing was done by the Indians, in retaliation for the death of the lone Pavhant, but Washington thought otherwise. The Mormons hated the US government, hated the federal surveys of Mormon lands. The Mormons were convinced that the gentiles were at it again, planning the extinction of the Mormons in devious and long-range ways.

The government in Washington thought that the Mormons had killed the surveyors, a typical Mormon thing to do, from the perspective of Washington, maybe by using the Indians to do the dirty work, but all the same. The Mormons were friendly with the Indians, training them in whiteskin ways.

The Walker War was morphing into the Utah War, the Mormons under attack from two sides. The Indians and the federal government squeezing Zion to a bursting point.

Incident at the Pond House

2001, November, cold and rainy, a lousy day. Everyone was cooped up in the new house, ten in the morning, maybe eleven. I had plans to play tennis, indoor tennis, in the afternoon. Lucky me.

Sheila had gone stir crazy. She said, "I have to get out of here. Let's get in the car, go somewhere, look at something."

"How about Washington," I said. "We can look at the White House and have dinner." Washington, D.C., is sixty-five miles away, one of the benefits of life in Gettysburg. I called my friends and canceled out of tennis.

The little ones got into the car, but Melanie refused, for no perceptible reason. Sheila pleaded and reasoned and cajoled. I pleaded and reasoned and cajoled. Melanie spit and hissed and ran away to hide. I found her upstairs in a closet. She ran again. The house is huge, thirteen rooms, an attic, a basement, two staircases, many places to hide. I was getting angry. *I* was simmering, the character I call *I*, simmering and wanting to emerge. Sheila was already angry.

I looked in the other closets, the other bedrooms, went up to the attic, searched through the attic, found her way in the back, at the bottom of the other staircase, curled up beside a sealed door. Her eyes flashed in the dark. She refused to come out.

I went down to get her. The staircase is narrow, hasn't been used in years. I grabbed her by the wrist, tried to get her to stand up. She resisted. I put my hands beneath her arms and pulled her stumblingly up the stairs.

She fought with me. Her nails were long, like claws, and she dug them into my forearms. I held on, decided she could not be in charge, picked her up. She screamed and wailed, said she was going to call the authorities.

As I carried her toward the front staircase, she continued to fight and scratch, a feral cat. I grabbed her hands to stop the scratching. I squeezed her hands, then squeezed them harder. The other *I* wanted to throw her to the floor, but I concentrated on breathing.

I carried her outside and got her in the car. By the time we reached Frederick, thirty miles away, she was acting like the other herself. When we crossed the first street in Washington, I felt her take my hand.

The Mormon Reformation

Spring 1854. President Pierce sent Lieutenant Colonel Edward J. Steptoe and his band of soldiers to Utah to investigate the Gunnison killings. Then in the fall, Pierce decided to replace Brigham as governor. He asked Steptoe to serve, but Steptoe said no. The move would be incendiary. He recommended that Brigham be left in power.

1855, the Mormons reached an agreement with the Pavhants. Seven Indians would be tried for the Gunnison killings, three who had actually participated and four the chief thought expendable. The jury would be composed of Mormons. The judge would be a gentile, a federal appointee.

At the end of the trial, the judge charged the jury to find the Indians guilty of first-degree murder. The Mormon jury found the three guilty of manslaughter and set the others free. A few days later the guilty ones conveniently escaped when their Mormon guards were looking away with spiritual sight or playing cards or praying.

Colonel Steptoe suspected a conspiracy, a Mormon challenge to the federal government. He wrote letters to Washington denouncing the territorial secretary, Almond Babbitt, who had served as the principal attorney for the defense. Meanwhile, President Pierce had appointed two new judges openly hostile to the Mormons. George Stiles was an apostate, an excommunicated Mormon, an adulterer. The other, Willis Drummond, had abandoned his wife and children in Illinois and arrived in Utah with a prostitute.

Things turned worse in 1856. Sensing complacency among the Mormons, religious complacency, Brigham and the leaders began the Mormon Reformation, the reinvigoration of devotion to the faith. Brigham exhorted the bishops to preach fire and brimstone, to confront sinners and backsliders and demand that they confess. John Doyle Lee explained what might happen then: "If the confession was not full and complete...[and] unless...repentance immediately followed, the sinful member was to be slain for the remission of his sins, it being taught by the leaders and believed by the people that the right thing to do with a sinner who did not repent and obey the council, was to take the life of the offending party, and thus save his everlasting soul. This was called 'Blood Atonement.'"

1857, early in the year. Brigham mentioned the doctrine of blood atonement in a sermon: "This is loving our neighbor as ourselves; if he needs help, help him; if he wishes salvation, and it is necessary to spill his blood upon the ground in order that he be saved, spill it."

Early March, still in 1857. William Parrish and his two sons, Beeson and Orrin, having lost their faith, wanted to leave the kingdom. They were attacked by the Danites, and William and Beeson were slain. Orrin escaped and complained to the officials, but no charges were filed.

1857, late March, the thirtieth. Judge Willis Drummond wrote a letter to Jeremiah Black, attorney to the new president, James Buchanan. In the words of historian Thomas G. Alexander,

> The letter charged the Saints with treason, disloyalty, and violence against the American people and government.... He said that they recognized no law superior to the Mormon prophet's commands. He charged that a secret oath-bound band—the Danites, or Destroying Angels—took the lives and property of anyone who questioned the church. He

said that such assassins had killed Gunnison....

In a peroration, he wrote that "the Federal officers are daily compelled to hear the form of the American government traduced, the chief executives of the nation, both dead and living, slandered and abused...in the most vulgar, loathsome, and wicked manner that the evil passions of men can possibly conceive." Finally, he suggested that the president appoint a non-Mormon governor and send him to Utah with "a *sufficient* military aid."

President Buchanan had heard enough. He was ready to march against the Mormons.

Part V
Trouble on the Way

Trouble in Arkansas

1857, the thirteenth of May. Parley Pratt, close friend to Joseph, close friend to Brigham, one of the earliest apostles, was murdered by a gentile preacher in Arkansas, a Unitarian minister, the Reverend Hector McLean.

Parley had taken a wife, his umpteenth wife, in Salt Lake City, Eleanor McLean, a comely convert recently arrived from Arkansas. Eleanor had a preacher husband back in Arkansas, a gentile husband and a passel of children. Parley and Ellen went back to Arkansas to get the children.

The preacher was not happy. He pulled Parley from his wagon and stabbed him many times. He stabbed him in the back, in the chest, and in the neck. Parley Pratt's lifeblood oozed from his body in the Arkansas sun while his newest wife watched, shrieked, and fled.

Eleanor headed back to Utah alone, without her kids.

We Buy Some Skates

The first winter the new family lived in Pennsylvania, the winter of 2000–2001, was a hard one. Our climate is generally mild. We live east of the mountains, east of the Appalachians, at the western end of the coastal plain. The worst of winter normally lasts about a month, but that winter, the first one we spent at the Pond House, was a hard one, and the pond froze early.

The girls were happy in the cold. They played on the pond, put on coats and hats and mittens and boots and played in the snow and on the pond. Crystal came back in the house and yelled some words that included my name. "Come upstairs if you want to talk to me," I yelled right back.

She clomped up the stairs and into my home office. "Hey, Peter, can we go skating on the pond?"

"Do you know how to skate?"

"No, but we can learn," she said.

"Do you have skates?"

"No, but you can buy us some."

"Oh," I said.

I loved to skate, back in the old days. Back in Minnesota when I was a kid, we skated day and night in the winter, my sister and I. It would be a great thing to skate again, to skate with Sheila and the girls. We would live a Norman Rockwell life, the whole ideal thing. We would fish in the summer and skate in the winter. We would bob for apples and drink hot chocolate. We would wear bib overalls and till the ground and go to the county fair.

I went out to the garage, to the little red barn that we use for a garage and for storage. I dug through boxes and found my skates, the skates I had last worn in Vermont, twenty-five years ago. My skates still fit. I gathered the troops, the soon-to-be skaters. I took them to stores, first to Wal-Mart's everything store then to Dick's Sporting Goods store, and bought four pairs of skates.

Trouble in Washington and Missouri

1857, the twentieth of May. President James Buchanan decided that he had heard enough. Brigham had to go. A new governor, a gentile governor with power to veto, had to be found and appointed. Absolute power to veto any Mormon decision. The president began looking for just the right man.

May 28, 1857. President Buchanan sent an order to the army commander at Fort Leavenworth in Colorado. *Assemble a force of twenty-five hundred men. Have them ready to escort the new governor to Utah, ready as soon as I find the right man.*

June, 1857, the middle of the month. Abraham O. Smoot arrived at the post office in Independence, Missouri, to pick up the monthly mail waiting to be carried west. Abraham's company, a Mormon company, had a contract with the US government to carry the mail to Salt Lake City and points beyond.

Abraham did not get the mail this day. He and his Mormon company received a pink slip instead. The government of the United States of America had canceled the contract, on orders from President Buchanan. Abraham left that day to bring the news to Salt Lake City.

1857, June, at the tail end of the month. President Buchanan found his man. He chose Alfred Cummings, a gentile from the state of Georgia, to replace Brigham Young as governor of the Utah Territory. Cummings headed off to Colorado, to Fort Leavenworth. By the time in the middle of July, the army contingent was ready to go.

Some Mormons were there, watching the preparations. One of them hurried away to the west, to Salt Lake City, carrying the news: *President Buchanan's invading gentile force was on its way to Utah.*

We Skate on the Pond

We walked out to the pond in our boots, sat down on the hill, and put on our skates. I went from person to person tightening the laces. Sheila skated once. One little skate-step on the pond, and then she was done with skating, forever. Sheila grew up in Phoenix, and skating was not for her. Bring on the bright lights. Bring on the desert winds. "I'll be in the kitchen, making hot chocolate," she said, walking back up the hill.

We skated, the girls and I. In a manner of speaking, we skated. I was rusty. I did not fall down, but I wobbled. Melanie learned fast, the oldest girl, ten years old. She skated across the pond. She skated around the pond. She was relentless, skating all the time, never falling down.

Crystal was determined, eight years old. She ran on her skates, ran across the pond on her ankles and her skates. For ten steps, maybe eight or twelve, then she was down and sliding on her belly. Then she was up and running on her skates, her skates and her ankles, for ten steps, or eight or twelve. Then she was back on her belly, sliding across the pond. This went on for hours.

Rebekkah sat on her butt, seven years old. She tried to skate a couple of times, then sat down on her butt and began drawing pictures in the snow on the ice. Occasionally she would crawl across the ice, get up, try to skate again, then fall on her butt and start to draw.

Melanie thought she was good. She wanted to race with the hot shot from Minnesota, the hot-shot with the wobbling glide. "Hah!" I said. "You wanna race with me? You goin' down, girl!"

We raced. We started in the middle of the pond and headed toward the edge. Melanie took an early lead. I wobbled along behind. I caught up, almost even. We were skate to skate. Then Melanie cut in front of me. I wobbled into her and went down, like a tree. Like a majestic ancient elm tree from back in Minnesota.

I landed on my left side. I tucked in my elbow to protect my ribs. I landed on my elbow and bruised my ribs. Melanie was celebrating her win by skating around me and laughing. She pointed in my face and sang, "Peter is a loser, Peter is a loser." I lay on the ice, gasping for air.

The News Arrives in Salt Lake City

1857, the twenty-third of June. Eleanor Pratt, formerly Eleanor McLean, arrived in Salt Lake City with news of her newest husband's death. She described the stabbing in detail, the blood oozing out of the body, the sight of her husband face down in the Arkansas dirt.

Parley Pratt, Mormon divine, one of the earliest converts, apostle to both Joseph and Brigham, had been murdered in Arkansas by a typically vicious Arkansas gentile preacher.

Sheila Mulligan and Crystal Webb

July, 1857, the twenty-fourth, Pioneer Day, the tenth anniversary of the arrival in Utah. The Mormons were gathered at the head of Big Cottonwood Canyon to celebrate. Brigham would speechify and preach. Many others would speechify and preach. Much food and drink would be consumed.

Back in Salt Lake City, in the middle of the same day, two breathless messengers arrived. Abraham Smoot arrived from Independence, Missouri, with news that the government had canceled the mail contract. Another man arrived from Colorado, from Fort Leavenworth, with news of the invading army.

Four men mounted fresh horses and galloped up Big Cottonwood Canyon with the news. Abraham Smoot, Orrin Porter Rockwell, and two others. They dismounted by the platform where Brigham was speaking. Invasion is imminent, they said. A federal army is on its way to the Utah Territory. Brigham Young is to be replaced by a new governor. The mail contract has been canceled. The United States is taking control of Utah.

Brigham changed his tune, spoke again to the crowds. *The gentiles are coming again. Burning, murder, and rape are at hand. We must prepare for war.*

He ordered all the Mormon people from the outer settlements to come into the forts and towns. He decreed that the United States Army must not be allowed to enter the territory.

1857, early August. Orrin Porter Rockwell led a contingent of militia fighters to Colorado. They killed stray army horses, burned standing army wagons, felled trees to block the trails. The army was stalled to the point where winter would keep it from Utah.

The fourth of August, 1857. On this day Brigham Young sent George A. Smith to the south to rally the Mormons. A fiery speaker Smith spoke against the invading army, encouraged the men to defend their towns. He spoke of the presence of strangers from back east, some from Missouri and Illinois, some from Arkansas, gentile strangers. Strangers who might be spies, gentile scouts spying on behalf of the invading enemy.

All these people, soldiers and civilians alike, had to be watched.

Had to be fought. The Mormons must be ready to protect their land, their territory, their way of life. The gentiles were coming to wipe out the saints. *The horrors of Missouri and Illinois must not be allowed to happen again. If gentiles have to die, then gentiles have to die.*

Melanie and ADHD

2000–2001, 2001–2002. Melanie was in fourth grade that first year we lived in the Pond House. She had not done well in school in Salt Lake City, so we decided she would repeat fourth grade. She was assigned to the right teacher, surely by chance, just the right teacher for a girl like Melanie.

Melanie would sit at her desk and play with her things, with her books, her papers, her pens and pencils, moving them around on the desk, putting them into the storage area beneath the desktop and taking them out again. The teacher would give an assignment. Melanie would be playing with her things or whispering to a friend, the girl in the desk next door.

Melanie was flunking fourth grade. She was not writing her assignments in her agenda book, was not doing the assignments she did not write down, was not turning in the assignments she managed to hear about and do.

The teacher called the parents, invited them in for a conference. Melanie could not pay attention, was constantly distracted, not by others but by herself. Was she like this at home? Distracted, maybe hyperactive, hard to control, subject to sudden, abrupt, unexpected changes? Yes, yes, yes, yes, yes, and yes. "Hmm," said the teacher. "Have you thought that she might have ADHD?"

"ADHD," said Sheila, "you mean attention deficit hyperactivity disorder?"

"Yes," said the teacher. "She looks like a classic case to me. You might want to have her tested."

Sheila took Melanie to the doctor and had her tested. "Looks like ADHD to me," said the doctor. "She has all the classic symptoms. I suggest Aderol, a low dose to start with. We'll reevaluate and take it from there."

Melanie was with that teacher for two years, for fourth grade and fifth. Her progress was gradual but sure. By the end of fifth grade she was off the medicine and doing fine, filling out her agenda book every day and doing her homework most nights. Sometimes she would backslide, not get something done. We diagnosed her as normal, a typical eleven-year-old girl.

The Fancher Party Reaches Utah

Migration was still going on, more robustly than ever, migration from east to west, from the Midwest to the far West. From New York and West Virginia, from Illinois and Kentucky, from Missouri and Arkansas, all the way to California, to the Oregon Territory, to a better, brighter place.

The Fancher Party had started out from Arkansas in May or June. By July they were in Colorado, crossing the Rocky Mountains, following roughly the trail the Mormons had started following ten years earlier and had been following ever since.

On August the fourth, 1857, the Fancher Party arrived in Salt Lake City, on that day or one close by, a group of pioneers getting a late start for the west. Late in the year. They needed to hurry, needed to take a safe route, the route south from Salt Lake City. The Donner Party had started late and gone straight west from Salt Lake City, had frozen and eaten one another in the mountains. The Fancher Party would head south.

Peer Mediators

2001, fall, our second fall in the Pond House. Melanie and Crystal were both attending Lincoln Elementary, Melanie in fifth grade, Crystal in fourth. They both signed up to be peer mediators, peacemakers, interveners, sprinklers of oil on troubled waters. Crystal ended up quitting halfway through the year, but Melanie stuck it out.

Early in the fall, they went through training, training to be peer mediators. One night after dinner they wanted to practice. They told Sheila and me to have an argument. We decided to argue about whose turn it would be to take the dog out in the middle of the night, Daisy, the Bernese Mountain Dog. We had bought her the previous spring. She was still a puppy in the fall. Taking her out in the middle of the night was something Sheila and I argued about for real.

We sat on the couch, pretending to argue. The girls approached. Each of them had a script. Melanie read from her script. "I see that you are having a conflict. Do you need a peer mediator?"

"Yes," said Sheila. "He is being mean."

I said, "No." I reminded her and them that I took the dog out last night. I said, "Tonight is her turn."

Crystal read from her script. "It sounds like you do need a peer mediator." They were doing a team intervention. They were taking turns talking.

"Peter," said Melanie, "what are your feelings right now?"

"I want to gouge her eyes out," I said. I was playing it for laughs.

"Sheila," said Melanie, "what are your feelings…"

"Hey!" said Crystal. "It's my turn! I'm supposed to ask that!"

"You always think it's your turn," replied Melanie.

"I do not, cheater," said Crystal. And she grabbed Melanie by the hair. Melanie smacked Crystal in the chops. Crystal pulled Melanie down to the floor. Melanie grabbed Crystal by the throat. Sheila yelled, "Stop it!" I asked the girls if they needed a peer mediator.

That happened in the fall of 2001. Here in the Pond House. My second success at being a mediator.

To the South: To Mountain Meadows

The Fancher Party were the wrong people, Arkansans, arriving in the wrong place, Utah, at the wrong time, when the Mormons were expecting invasion from the East. With them they carried a bad attitude and a bad group of helpers.

The party itself consisted of eleven families, twenty-two adults with twenty-nine children and fourteen other adults. An unrelated group of men traveled with them, pulling the supply wagons, driving the cattle, doing the hard work. These men called themselves the Missouri Wildcats and were proud of their hatred of Mormons. Some of them had fought the Mormons back in Missouri, and now they boasted of what they had done then, hinted at what they might do again.

The Mormons responded with hostility, refusing to trade with the travelers, refusing to sell them provisions, refusing to let them graze their cattle on Mormon land. A member of another party that arrived shortly after the Fancher Party described the situation: "We came on to Buttermilk Fort…and found the inhabitants greatly enraged at the train which had just passed, declaring that they had abused the Mormon women, calling them w–s, etc., and letting on about the men. The people had refused to sell that train any provisions, and told us they were sorry they had not killed them there; but they knew it would be done before they got in."

The Fancher Party arrived in Cedar City, in the southwest corner of Utah, in early September. They were in a weakened state, hungry, and weary from a series of skirmishes with the Indians. They traveled a few miles farther west and camped in a place called Mountain Meadows, seeking rest for the people, grass and water for the cattle and horses.

Isaac C. Haight was president of the stake in Cedar City. On the sixth of September, 1857, shortly after the party had passed through, he reminded his people of the treatment they had received back east:

> They drove us out to starve. When we pled for mercy, Haun's Mill was our answer, and when we asked for bread they gave us a stone. We left the confines of civilization and came far into the wilderness where we could worship God according to the dictates of our own conscience without annoyance to our neighbors. We resolved that if they would leave us alone we would never trouble them. But the Gentiles will

not leave us alone. They have followed us and hounded us. They come among us asking us to trade with them, and in the name of humanity to feed them. All of this we have done and now they are sending an army to exterminate us. So far as I am concerned I have been driven from my home for the last time. I am prepared to feed to the Gentiles the same bread they fed to us.

The Indians attacked the Fancher Party on that day, maybe on their own and maybe in collusion with the Mormons. They surrounded the migrants and kept them under siege for the next five days. Several of the pioneers were killed, some trying to escape. Food grew scarce in the camp and ammunition ran low. During the siege the Mormons were meeting. The leaders were watching the conflict and planning their strategy.

Melanie and Football

2002, sometime in the fall, our third fall in the Pond House. Melanie came to me one day and said, "Peter, will you buy me a football?"

"Huh?" I said. All I could think of to say at first was "Huh?" Then I said, "Why? You're a girl. Girls don't play football. Why do you want a football?"

"We've been playing football at school, in gym class. I'm really good at throwing the ball, and I want to play football with you."

We went to Wal-Mart, and I bought her a football, a smaller one, a football that would fit her hand and be easy to throw. We went to the field behind the little red barn we use as a garage and played catch. She could throw a perfect spiral, most of the time in my direction. When I threw it back, I made her run, first to one side or the other, then in various patterns. She had sure hands. She scored a lot of touchdowns.

Many evenings after dinner that fall, Melanie would say to me, "Let's go play catch." By the time winter began, she was throwing perfect spirals for thirty-yard gains, most of the time in my direction.

Innocent Blood

Diabolical as the plan was, it was perfectly carried out.
                                              —Juanita Brooks

John Doyle Lee was at the meetings, a prominent member of the Mormon community in the South. He kept a diary for all his years as a Mormon. Later, sitting in prison awaiting his execution, he wrote a book, a record of his days, his *Confessions.* He was at the final meeting before the massacre. He arrived late, but he heard the plan:

> I was then told the plan of action had been agreed upon, and it was this: The emigrants were to be decoyed from their stronghold under a promise of protection. Brother William Bateman was to carry a flag of truce and demand a parley, and then I was to go and arrange the terms of the surrender. I was to demand that all the children who were so young they could not walk should be put into a wagon, and the wounded were also to be put into a wagon. Then all the arms and ammunition of the emigrants should be put into a wagon, and I was to agree that the Mormons would protect the emigrants from the Indians and conduct them to Cedar City in safety, where they should be protected until an opportunity came for sending them to California.
>
> It was agreed that when I had made the full agreement and treaty, as the brethren called it, the wagons should start for Hamblin's Ranch with the arms, the wounded and the children. The women were to march on foot and follow the wagons in single file; the men were to follow behind the women, they also to march in single file. Major John M. Higbee was to stand with his militia company about two hundred yards from the camp, and stand in double file, open order, with about twenty feet space between the files, so that the wagons could pass between them. The drivers were to keep right along, and not stop at the troops. The women were not to stop there, but to follow the wagons. The troops

were to halt the men for a few minutes, until the women were some distance ahead, out into the cedars, where the Indians were hid in ambush. Then the march was to be resumed, the troops to form in single file, each soldier to walk by an emigrant, and on the right-hand side of his man, and the soldier was to carry his gun on his left arm, ready for instant use. The march was to continue until the wagons had passed beyond the ambush of the Indians, and until the women were right in the midst of the Indians. Higbee was then to give the orders and words, *"Do Your Duty."* At this the troops were to shoot down the men; the Indians were to kill all of the women and larger children, and the drivers of the wagons and I were to kill the wounded and sick men that were in the wagons. Two men were to be placed on horses near by, to overtake and kill any of the emigrants that might escape from the first assault. The Indians were to kill the women and large children, so that it would be certain that no Mormon would be guilty of shedding *innocent blood*—if it should happen that there was any innocent blood in the company that were to die. Our leading men said that there was no innocent blood in the whole company.

1857, September the eleventh. The Fancher Party was exterminated by the Mormons. On nine-eleven, the eleventh day of the ninth month in the year 1857, all of the members of the party except the babies—the women, the children, and the men—were killed, the Missouri Wildcats killed along with them. Their bodies were left to rot in the hot Utah sun.

Part VI
Truth and Falsehood

The Difference Between True and False

My father had a saying. "If it ain't, it oughta be." My father would tell a tale, maybe a tall tale. Someone would ask him, "Is that true?" My father would answer, "If it ain't, it oughta be." My father was kidding around. He knew the difference between true and false.

Did the Mormons know the difference? The old-time Mormon historians, the Mormon apologists and myth-makers, the Mormon hagiographers, the perpetrators of falseness in the history of Mormonism? Did they know the difference between true and false, between fact and fiction? Sometimes the answer is no.

Some Mormon history is based on faith rather than knowledge, knowledge of the facts. An excess of faith can be an excess of ignorance, ignorance of reality, of human nature, of the sources and the nature of evil.

The Mormons are God's chosen people. In the eyes of the Mormons, this is so. In the eyes of the faith-based Mormon historian, whatever the Mormons did reflects the will of God, and is right and true. Some Mormon falsehood grows from faith, from faith and innocence, from faith, innocence, and ignorance. This kind of Mormon falsehood is not intentional. It grows out of the ignorance that is a necessary component of faith.

In faith-based Mormon history, the false way is the only way it could be. God had said so. God had chosen his people. His people were innocent, just, right, and true. Whatever they did was right and true. If the Mormons did something that was not right and true, then they must have done something else. The false way is the way it had to be, the only way it could be.

But sometimes the answer is yes. Sometimes the apologist Mormon historian did know the difference between true and false. In the eyes of some Mormon historians, the Mormons had to be innocent even when they were guilty.

This kind of Mormon falsehood grows from guilt. Sometimes Mormon history is a creation of innocence based on known guilt.

Some Mormon historians have lied, revised the history, replaced it with a myth. For the good of the church itself, for the good of the faith. Sometimes the way Mormons had acted was not good in the sense of goodness, of innocence, of virtue. Then Mormon history had to be revised, rewritten until it looked good, translated from what reality had scratched onto the surface of the earth. These historians put their faces into their hats and looked into peep stones. Through the lens of spiritual vision, they discovered that the Mormon actors had actually been innocent bystanders, victims themselves. The dirty deeds had been committed by somebody else.

Then the Mormon historian could use my father's saying. Were someone to ask this kind of Mormon historian, *Is your story true,* he could answer, *If it ain't, it oughta be.*

Chicanery Happens

A cool afternoon in October, 2002, the twenty-first, one month after the autumnal equinox and two months before the winter solstice. Melanie gets home at 3:00. She leaves home at 6:45 in the morning, on the bus, headed for school. She is in middle school, sixth grade now, and her days are long, eight hours. She gets home at 3:00 every weekday afternoon.

She comes into the house and looks to see if I am here. We need to play catch, with the football. We need to play horse/pig, with the basketball. We need to go for a walk, take the dog on a long walk. We need to walk and talk.

Today she went to the phone first thing. She spent forty-five minutes on the phone with Megan, Megan the Vegan. Megan is still grounded, but now only from us.

A month and a half ago there was a dance at the middle school. Melanie and Megan were planning to go, but Megan's mom said no. Megan's mom runs a beauty parlor and goes to a fundamentalist church on Chambersburg Road, where dancing is sinful.

The girls came up with a plan. Megan would lie to her mom, would say she was going to spend the night here at our house, at the Pond House. Just spend the night with Melanie at the Pond House.

Maybe her mom would ask, *What about the dance?* Megan would answer, *What dance?* That look of pure blonde innocence on her face. Megan's mom fell for it. Unless she was dissembling, pretending to fall for it so she could trap the girls committing two sins. The sin of dancing, the sin of lying.

Sheila drove the girls to the dance. Sheila is Melanie's mother, and she drove Melanie and Megan to and from the dance.

Did Sheila know about the plan, about the chicanery that was under way? Sheila knew, but she had checked out the dance. It was just a dance, a bunch of twelve-year-olds. Sheila had no problem with dancing.

Sheila would escort the girls to the door before the dance. She would pick them up at the door after the dance. The girls would sleep at our house, and Megan's mom would never know. Sheila had joined the plan, had become the third sinner.

The girls had a great time. Megan's mom did not call during the dance to check on Megan. Sheila picked them up. The plan had worked like a dream. The three of them had a good laugh about it back at the Pond House.

Blame It on the Indians

The cover-up of the massacre arose from innocence. From a desire for innocence, a desire to remain innocent, to be thought innocent. The Mormons knew they had done wrong when they slaughtered the Fancher Party. Men, women, children. The Mormons knew they had done wrong, and now they had a problem, a bigger problem. The problem that had been growing for years had just become bigger.

President Buchanan was already suspicious and angry. He had chosen a new governor and had started the army on its way. Now the gentile emigrants were dead, their bodies rotting in the sun.

The Mormons who had been involved knew they had a problem, the leaders and the soldiers from the South. They gathered to discuss it. President Buchanan must not find out who had really killed the emigrants. History had to be rewritten.

They decided to blame the Indians. In the words of John Doyle Lee: "We pledged ourselves to keep everything relating to the affair a secret during life. We also took the most binding oaths to stand by each other, and to always insist that the massacre was committed by the Indians alone. This was the advice of Brigham Young."

Later there was some talk. Some of the brethren said a thing or two about the massacre, about who may have been there. Brigham himself traveled south, to preach and restore order, silence, and discipline. He reminded the men of their oath: "I am told that there are many of the brethren who are willing to inform upon and swear against the brethren who were engaged in that affair.... if there is,...you will die a *dog's* death, and be *damned*, and go to hell. I do not want to hear of any more *treachery among my people.*"

There was a massacre. The Mormons massacred the Fancher Party. Then there was a lie, an agreement to blame the Mountain Meadows Massacre on the Indians. The lie was a cover-up based on death and backed by Brigham's threat of death. More death.

Layers of Grounding

The telephone rang the next morning, the morning after the dance. Megan's mom was calling to talk to Sheila. She had figured it out, or she had been dissembling, had known it all along. One way or another, she knew that Megan had gone to the dance.

Megan's mom played it cool, asked if the girls had gone to the dance. Sheila said yes, she had taken the girls to and from the dance. The girls had had a great time. Megan's mom said she had forbidden Megan to go to the dance. Sheila said, "Uh-oh." Megan's mom explained her values, her theological objection to dancing. She asked if Sheila understood. Sheila said, "I understand."

Megan's mom thanked Sheila for understanding. Then she ordered Megan home. Megan went home and was grounded, for a month, General Grounding, from all activities except home and school and church.

Now that month is over. Megan's grounding ended on this cool afternoon in October. I was up here writing, waiting for Melanie to get home from school. She got off the bus and went straight to the phone, called Megan and asked her to come over. "Let's celebrate the end of your grounding."

Megan said no, she could not come over. Her mom had imposed a second month of grounding, Special Grounding, from our house only. For another month Megan may not come over to our house, to the Pond House, the house of dancing and evil.

Einstein had the Theory of Relativity, General Relativity, and Special Relativity. Megan's mom has the Theory of Grounding, General Grounding, and Special Grounding, Megan's grounding and our grounding. This is the month we are grounded from Megan.

We think of Megan as our fourth daughter, as one of ours. I call her Megan the Vegan, making the words rhyme. I do not say VEE-gan, I say VEH-gan, so the word rhymes with Megan. I have a song I sing whenever she comes over. I sing to the tune of "Devil or Angel," a song from the old days. It goes, "Megan the Vegan / Why won't you eat your meat? / A balanced meal / Includes a bite of meat." I don't mean much of anything. The song is my way of saying hello, saying hello to Megan the Vegan.

It gets her goat. When I sing my song, Megan laughs and sputters, laughs and complains, laughs and whines. "Peter!" she says. "I am not a vegan! I do eat meat."

I reply to her protest with a rhetorical question, an irrefutable question. I ask, "Then why is your name Megan? Megan rhymes with vegan. If you are not a vegan, then why is your name Megan?"

She says her name is Ashley. Megan is just her middle name. Her real name is Ashley, so she must not be a vegan.

"I Did Not Know There Were So Many"

He had not known because he had not taken the trouble to know. He was satisfied with what he did not know. Knowing more was inconvenient and frightening.... And all he could say was that he did not know. He was guilty, therefore, of innocence. [Is] there anything so loathsome as a willfully innocent man? Hardly. An innocent man is a sin before God. Inhuman and therefore unworthy. No man should live without absorbing the sins of his kind, the foul air of his innocence, even if it did wilt rows of angel trumpets and cause them to fall off their vines.

—Toni Morrison

Colonel Dame was an innocent man, Colonel William H. Dame, head of the militia in Cedar City in 1857, the Mormon militia for all of southern Utah. Lieutenant Colonel Isaac C. Haight, president of the local stake, was his second in command, above Major John M. Higbee. John Doyle Lee was there at the gathering of the militia when Major Higbee arrived with the plan:" All the emigrants must be *put out of the way*. President Haight has counseled with Colonel Dame or had orders from him to put all of the emigrants out of the way; none who are old enough to talk are to be spared."

Higbee participated in the massacre. Early the next morning Dame and Haight arrived at Jacob Hamblin's ranch near the Meadows. John Doyle Lee was there, sleeping on the floor:

I was awakened by loud talking between Isaac O. Haight and William H. Dame. They were very much excited, and quarreling with each other. I got up at once, but was unable to hear what they were quarreling about, for they cooled down as soon as they saw that others were paying attention to them....

After breakfast we all went back in a body to the Meadows, to bury the dead and take care of the property that was left there.

When we reached the Meadows we all rode up to that part of the field where the women were lying dead. The bodies of the men, women, and children had been stripped entirely naked, making the scene one of the most loathsome and ghastly that can be imagined....

Colonel Dame was silent for some time. He looked all over the field, and was quite pale, and looked uneasy and frightened. I thought then that he was just finding out the difference between giving and executing orders for whole-sale killing. He spoke to Haight, and said:

"I must report this matter to the authorities."

"How will you report it?" said Haight.

Dame said, "I will report it just as it is."

"Yes, I suppose so, and implicate yourself with the rest?" said Haight.

"No," said Dame. "I will not implicate myself, for I had nothing to do with it."

Haight then said, "That will not do, for you know a d**d sight better. You ordered it done. Nothing has been done except by your orders, and it is too late in the day for you to order things done and then go back on it, and go back on the men who have carried out your orders. You cannot *sow pig* on me, and I will be d**d if I will stand it. You are as much to blame as any one, and you know that we have done nothing except what you ordered done. I know that I have obeyed orders, and by G*d I will not be lied on."

Colonel Dame was much excited. He choked up, and would have gone away, but he knew Haight was a man of determination, and would not stand any foolishness.

As soon as Colonel Dame could collect himself, he said:

"I did not think there were so many of them, or I would not have had anything to do with it."

Haight stepped up to my side, a little in front of me, and facing Colonel Dame. He was very mad, and said:

"The trouble is just this: Colonel Dame *counseled* and *ordered* me to do this thing, and now he wants to back out, and go back on me, and by G*d, he shall not do it. He shall not lay it *all* on me. He cannot do it. He must not try to do it. I will *blow him to h**l* before he shall lay it all on me. He has got to stand up to what he did, like a little man. He knows he ordered it done, and I dare him to deny it."

Colonel Dame was perfectly cowed. He did not offer to deny it again, but said: "Isaac, I did not know there were so many of them."

Colonel Dame was an innocent man, a blustery innocent man, angry and impatient for action. He was innocent in the sense of being ignorant, of reality, of the damage that fierce action can cause in the hands of an innocent, ignorant man.

Cook Your Own Goose

Melanie talked with Megan for forty-five minutes. Right after getting home from school, right after saying goodbye to Megan and getting off the bus, Melanie asked Megan on the phone if she could come over.

Megan was not allowed to come over. She had been placed under Special Grounding. Melanie came to find me. If she could not hang out with Megan, she would have to hang out with me. We were to go outside to the driveway and the basketball goal and play horse/pig. She plays horse and I play pig. If I miss three shots that she has made, I lose. My three missed shots spell p-i-g. I am a pig. If she misses five shots that I have made, she loses. Her five missed shots spell h-o-r-s-e. She is a horse. This is how we make the game more fair. She gets five misses, I get three.

We play Cook Your Own Goose. One person will make a shot. If the other person makes the same shot, then the first person has to make the shot again. If she misses she gets a letter. This is called cooking your own goose, an optional feature to the game of horse/ pig. I love making Melanie cook her own goose. When I make the shot she made, I talk trash. I say, "Turn on the oven, Melanie! Pluck the feathers from that goose!" I tell her she is dead meat.

I am a trash talker. This is a fatherly thing. I am preparing her for real life.

Yaw Guts

John Doyle Lee was there, at the meadows. Through the whole thing, the Mountain Meadows Massacre. Afterward he stayed in the community, farmed his farms, raised his families, preached to his people in his church. Everyone else ran away, all the other leading players, to the mountains, to Nevada, to Arizona. Lee was advised to run away, by the prophet himself, Brigham Young. Lee did not run away. He stayed around and faced the music, endured the gossip, the rumors, the accusations. Eventually the Mormons brought him down, his people, the Mormons. Twenty years after the massacre, John Doyle Lee was made the Mormon scapegoat.

No one will ever know what he did. One can know what others said he did. One can know what he said he did and what he said he did not do. The rest is legend and speculation, stories made up in the cause of innocence or of guilt. Stories that are or are not true.

Here is one that is true. Shortly before the massacre, Lee confronted the Indians. He knew the Indians well. For many years he had been their agent, their protector, their teacher. He had learned their language, traded with them, taught them to farm. Now he found the Indians attacking the emigrants, the Fancher Party, at the Mountain Meadows.

"I heard the report of their guns, and the screams of the women and children in the corral," Lee said. He tried to put a stop to it:

> I ran with William Young and John Mangum, to where the Indians were, to stop the fight.... They fired a volley, and three balls from their guns cut my clothing.... I kept on until I reached the place where the Indians were in force. When

John Doyle Lee

I got to them, I told them the Great Spirit would be mad at them if they killed the women and children. I talked to them some time, and cried with sorrow when I saw that I could not pacify the savages.

When the Indians saw me in tears, they called me "Yaw Guts," which in the Indian language means "cry baby," and to this day [1877, twenty years later] they call me by that name and consider me a coward.

All the other sources agree that the Indians called Lee Yaw Guts. The Mormons who were there, who saw the whole thing, tell the same story. John Doyle Lee tells this story on himself, and everyone else agrees. It must be true. No hot-blooded Mormon warrior would make up a story, not a story like this one, branding himself a crying coward.

Lee looks like a truth teller to me. I have read his book. I have read the other books, the books of the historians, the biographers, the accounts told and written by Lee's enemies. I have studied the stories, the legends, the myths. In my opinion, John Doyle Lee told the truth. Tried to tell the truth. To the best of his knowledge, to the best of his ability to recall.

He kept a diary, for most of the days of his life. He wrote his *Confessions*, during his imprisonment, his last days, while awaiting his execution in his death cell. He had nothing to lose, nothing to gain, no reason to lie. He was still a Mormon, still believed in his god, knew his god was watching, listening, maybe even reading. Maybe Lee's god was reading while Lee was writing in the months, weeks, days, and hours leading up to his execution. John Doyle Lee, in no position not to tell the truth.

He tells the truth, John Doyle Lee, the man the Indians called Yaw Guts. I find this ironic. They called him Yaw Guts, the crybaby, the coward, but he was the only man brave enough to stay around, the only man honest enough to tell the truth, the only man strong enough to die for the sins of the Mountain Meadows Massacre. The man who stood before the firing squad and said, "Aim for my heart, boys." That man is the one the Indians called crybaby, called Yaw Guts, called coward.

His book is called *Mormonism Unveiled: The Life and Confessions of John D. Lee*. It was unavailable for many years, then reprinted in 2001 by Fierra Blanca Publications of Albuquerque, New Mexico, in a facsimile edition distributed by the University of New Mexico Press. *The Life and Confessions of John D. Lee* is my favorite book on the dark days of Mormonism. The paranoid days, the fundamentalist days, the murderous days, the days of unquestioning belief and misjudgment. The turbulent early days of Mormonism.

Fatherly-Daughterly Games

The other girls get home at 4:15, Crystal and Rebekkah. From elementary school, fifth grade and fourth. They leave at 8:15 and get home at 4:15, another long day, eight hours.

Melanie and I are playing horse/pig when the other girls get home. On that same cool day in October, October of 2002. We have started our second game. I won the first game, kicked her butt, taught her to spell h-o-r-s-e, taught her to cook her own goose.

When the other girls arrive, Melanie says she is done with basketball. We should go for a walk instead, a walk with the dog. Crystal says she would rather visit the cows. Rebekkah has already gone into the house. We cross the road and visit the cows. Crystal and I talk to them in cow talk. They look at us and pee.

Rebekkah comes out of the house and runs over to us. I say, "Melanie and I are going for a walk. Want to come?"

Rebekkah says no. "It's too cold out here, but give me a hug before you go." I give her a hug, and she and Crystal go back across the road to play in the Pond House.

We walk down Hilltown Road, Melanie and I, and turn left on Fairview Fruit Road, headed toward the place on the creek where we swim in the summer.

We have to walk past Megan's house. We do not see her, but we talk about her, about her and the dance, about the dance and about lying.

Lying is a big topic at the Pond House. I hear a lot of lies at the Pond House. The character I call *I* hears a lot of lies at the Pond House. Whoever *I* is. Maybe *I* is just I, just me. Maybe *I* and I are the same person after all. Maybe I am *I*.

There are two kinds of lies. General Lies and Special Lies. Special lies are rare at the Pond House. The dance would be an example of a Special Lie, a lie with one suspect. Megan said, "I am not going to the dance." Megan went to the dance and was busted. One person, one lie, an instance of the Special Lie.

General Lies are more common, in my life and Melanie's, much more common in our life at the Pond House. For example, the lie about my fountain pen, my second best fountain pen, the one I had owned for years. One day it was on my desk, and the next day it wasn't. This happened before the door and the lock. Before I replaced the missing door to my office and fitted it with a lock. Back when the three girls had access to my office, access unfettered by lock and door.

I kept the pen in a special place, ready for use, but now the pen had disappeared, had been taken by someone, by a person with criminal tendencies, by a criminal communist.

The disappearance of things was a too common mystery at the Pond House. I began to call the girls criminal communists. Sometimes I had reason to call them that.

The girls have criminal tendencies. They take stuff that is not theirs. The girls have communal tendencies. They stick together, through thick and thin, through good behavior and bad, against the enemy. They stick together against Sheila and me, against their mom and stepdad.

The girls are criminals. The girls are communists. The girls are criminal communists. One of the criminal communists had taken my fountain pen, my second-favorite fountain pen.

This much I knew, of this much I was certain. One of the criminal communists had stolen my pen. I interrogated Melanie. "No," said Melanie, "I did not take your pen." I interrogated Crystal. "No," said

Crystal, "I did not take your pen." I interrogated Rebekkah. "No,"
said Rebekkah, "I did not take your pen."

I interrogated them as a group. I said, "Someone took my pen."
I said, "One of you took my pen. Tell the truth and you won't get
in trouble." I said, "Which one of you took my pen?"

Melanie said, "It must have been Crystal. I would never take your
pen." Crystal said, "It must have been Melanie. I would never take
your pen." Rebekkah said, "It wasn't me. I did not take your pen."

No one had taken the pen. Everyone had taken the pen. It was
a criminal conspiracy, another instance of criminal communism,
another example of the General Theory of Lying. The Special
Theory says, *I did not do it.* The General Theory says, *No one did it.*
There is no one here but us angels. There are no onions in this
petunia patch.

Now it is today, and Melanie and I are walking, walking and
talking. I say the usual things. I say, "Lying is bad." I am referring
to the pen. I say, "Lying gets you grounded." I am referring to the
dance. I say, "Lying costs you friends." I say, "There is nothing to
be afraid of. Everyone does things wrong. It is best to say you did
it." I say, "I get angrier when you lie than when you do something
bad." I am doing my fatherly best.

Melanie says the usual things. She says, "I did not take your pen."
She says, "I know lying is bad. I know you'll be nice if I tell the truth."
She says, "I am telling the truth. I don't know who stole your pen."

Once she took a computer and gave it to her friend Olivia.
Sheila's old laptop that did not work anymore. Olivia's mother
called, and we got the laptop back. Now my pen is gone. Melanie
is not ready to change her wicked ways, but I am wearing her down,
toward adulthood, responsibility, good behavior.

We are on our walk, our long walk, our walk that goes on and
on. We are playing another of our games. We are playing a version
of cook your own goose. I am cooking my goose and she is cooking hers. She is cooking my goose and I am cooking hers. We are
cooking our geese. Walking down the road to the creek, we are

cooking our geese and playing a game, a fatherly-daughterly game.

What He Said He Did

Eventually they blamed it all on him. The idea, the planning, the execution of the plan. By the end they made it appear he had killed them all. All of the emigrants, everyone in the Fancher Party, the men, the women, the children. That is the story, the legend, the myth. John Doyle Lee did it all.

I will tell you what he said he did, in his *Confessions*, what John Doyle Lee, writing in his death cell, said he did during the Mountain Meadows Massacre. He says he was not in on the actual planning, but when the plan was explained to him, he agreed to do his part.

He was to be the spokesman, the facilitator. The Fancher Party was to be led out of the meadows, out of Utah. He told the emigrants what to do. Put the babies, the guns, the ammunition in one wagon. Put the wounded in another wagon. The women and the men would walk behind the wagons. "The Mormons would protect the emigrants from the Indians and conduct them to Cedar City in safety, where they should be protected until an opportunity came for sending them to California." Thus spake the facilitator, John Doyle Lee.

The wagons moved out. Lee moved out with the wagons. The women followed, then the men. The gentile men moved out in single file, each with an armed Mormon guard at his side, the Mormon troops. At a certain point, the immigrant men were stopped and the wagons went on, "into the cedars, where the Indians were hid in ambush." The Indians were there to kill the women. The Mormon guards stayed behind to kill the gentile men. "It was my duty, with the two drivers," wrote John Doyle Lee, "to kill the sick and wounded who were in the wagons, and to do so when we heard the guns of the troops fire."

So it nearly happened. The drivers were named McMurdy and Knight:

McMurdy was in front; his wagon was mostly loaded with the arms and small children. McMurdy and Knight got out of their wagons; each one had a rifle. McMurdy went up to Knight's wagon, where the sick and wounded were, and raising his rifle to his shoulder, said: "*O Lord, my God, receive their spirits, it is for thy Kingdom that I do this.*" He then shot a man who was lying with his head on another man's breast; the ball killed both men.

I also went up to the wagon, intending to do my part of the killing. I drew my pistol and cocked it, but somehow it went off prematurely, and I shot McMurdy across the thigh, my pistol ball cutting his buckskin pants. McMurdy turned to me and said:

"Brother Lee, keep cool, you are excited; you came very near killing me. Keep cool, there is no reason for being excited."

Knight then shot a man with his rifle; he shot the man in the head. Knight also brained a boy that was about fourteen years old.... By this time many Indians reached our wagons, and all of the sick and wounded were killed almost instantly.... I did not kill any one there, but it was an accident that kept me from it, for I fully intended to do my part of the killing, but by the time I got over the excitement of coming so near killing McMurdy, the whole of the killing of the wounded was done.

Lee knew his willingness to kill was the same as killing, in the eyes of his God. He does not spare himself. "I here pause in the recital of this horrid story of man's inhumanity and ask myself the question, is it honest in me, and can I clear my conscience before my God, if I screen myself while I accuse others? No, never! Heaven forbid that I should put a burden upon others' shoulders, that I am unwilling to bear my just portion of. I am not a traitor to my people, nor to my former friends and comrades who were with me on that dark day when the work of death was carried on in God's name, by a lot of deluded and religious fanatics. It is my duty to tell facts as they exist, and I will do so."

Atonement by Grounding

November now, the fourth, 2002, another cool day. 3:00 p.m. The bus from the middle school stops in front of the Pond House with lights flashing. Sheila and I are out there on the porch waiting for the mail.

We have been told not to be out front when the bus arrives. It embarrasses Melanie. She thinks we are treating her like a kindergartener. But our presence does not embarrass Megan, whose stop is later, around the corner on Fairview Fruit Road. We do not embarrass Megan the Vegan.

Megan looks out the window as Melanie exits the bus. Megan is sitting by the window, and she is waving to us. Megan the Vegan is waving excitedly through the tinted window, that look of pure blonde innocence all over her face.

She is still grounded from the Pond House, and we miss her. We regret the whole thing. Maybe not the dance, but the other stuff. The chicanery and the cover-up. We have learned an important lesson. We will never lie about sinfulness again. We are done with the rewriting of history. We want our fourth daughter to come over again.

Part VII
Pride and Perversity

The Earliest Years of John Doyle Lee

His mother was Elizabeth, Elizabeth Doyle at her birth, Elizabeth Doyle Reed in her first marriage, Elizabeth Doyle Lee in her second. In 1804 she married Oliver Reed, who was involved in a dispute with another man about a piece of land. On a night when the couple were sleeping, the other man entered their house, picked up the iron seat of a loom, and used it to kill Oliver. Elizabeth recognized the man and spoke his name. He struck her too, then the baby, little William Oliver Reed, and fled the house.

Elizabeth fled too, with both her children, back to her father's house in Kaskaskia, Illinois. She married Ralph Lee in 1811, gave birth to John Doyle Lee on the twelfth of September in 1812, fell ill in 1815 and died. Ralph Lee was a drinker, and from then on he drank and drank.

For the next four years, young John Doyle Lee was cared for by a nurse, a black woman who spoke only French. At the age of seven he was sent to live with his Uncle James and Aunt Charlotte: "I lived in [that] family eight years, and can safely say I got a whipping every day I was there.... My aunt was more like a savage than a civilized woman. In her anger she generally took her revenge upon those around her who were the least to blame. She would strike with anything she could obtain with which to work an injury. I [was] knocked down and beaten by her until I was senseless, scores of times, and I yet carry many scars on my person, the result of my harsh usage by her."

Fifty Years Ago, Maybe More

I was twelve years old, maybe thirteen—I, me, the author of this book. This is a story about my father, maybe the worst one I could tell about him, maybe not. He was a good guy, an amusing guy, my dad, as I think the story I told earlier shows, but he did not spend much time with me. Here is a small proof of that. Basketball was my game when I was a kid. I spent hours back of our house, on the dirt driveway to the garage, shooting baskets and dribbling around.

One evening my dad came home from work while I was out there in the Minnesota dusk, shooting. I opened the garage door for him to pull in his car, then went back to my game. After he emerged, he watched for a minute, then asked for the ball, bounced it once, and swished a two-handed set shot from fifteen feet. Having never imagined he could do such a thing, I looked at him stunned in amazement. "You didn't think I could do that, did you?" he asked, then went into the house. He never did it again, and he never explained.

So now I am thirteen years old, maybe twelve. I rode my bike to the house of some kid I did not know with another kid from my neighborhood that I hardly knew. This happened at night. The last name of the kid from my neighborhood may have been Rosen, but it also may not have been. This is a long time ago, 1952 or 1953. The house we went to was a couple of miles away, beyond the big hill on Fifty-Third Street.

The three of us stood around in the other kid's yard, talking and idly pushing a tire swing around, as though we were playing catch with a ball. When I happened to be looking away for some reason or other, the tire came my way and hit the back of my left hand, breaking a bone. It hurt like crazy.

I got on my bike and headed home. When I arrived at the top of the hill on Fifty-Third Street, I stopped, knowing I could not steer, keep my balance, and control my speed going down that hill with only one hand on the handlebar.

A car pulled up. Tom McBurney, a high school kid, three or four years older, got out, asked me what was wrong, put my bike in his trunk, and took me home.

My parents argued about what to do. My mother thought we should go to the emergency room, but my father was already in bed and not to be bothered. I was sitting in misery and pain—and yes, crying—on the floor in the hallway outside their bedroom when my father emerged to go to the bathroom. I asked him again if we could do something, and he again said no, and I muttered the word "bastard," and he hit me on the side of my face with the back of his hand and bounced my head off the wall.

I did not sleep that night. In the morning we went to the emergency room, where I got an x-ray and a cast.

A couple of weeks later I was at a high school baseball game. An older kid came by, looked at my cast, asked "Did she roll over on you?" and walked on. I had no idea what he was talking about, but if I had, the answer would have been no.

"This Proud, Perverse Streak in His Nature"

With three months only of formal education, John Doyle Lee somehow learned to read and write, eventually taught himself to write well. He ran away from Aunt Charlotte's house at sixteen, succeeded at a series of jobs, nearly died a couple of times, fell in love, accumulated a grubstake, then went home to Kaskaskia to marry Emily, a motherless girl employed at a tavern.

He loitered in the tavern, playing cards with a group of gamblers who let him win often enough to keep him in the game. Emily watched his money draining away, said he should stop gambling, said she would not marry him until he did. He said he would stop when he was ready, but not if she told him to.

According to Juanita Brooks, Lee's biographer and kinsperson, "This proud, perverse streak in his nature kept him from making any concession, so…he left." Perhaps. Perhaps he left out of perversity.

Or perhaps he did it for the good of himself, for *pride* in himself. Perhaps he remembered Aunt Charlotte, the *perversity* of her savage rule. Pride is one thing. Perversity is another. *Proud* is a word Lee used to describe himself, often, sometimes with regret. *Perverse* is a word used in a sentence written by Juanita Brooks.

A Hundred-Dollar Bill, a Benjamin

Benjamin Franklin's face is on the hundred-dollar bill. I carry one in my wallet, for emergencies, have done so for years. One hundred dollars cash, a single Benjamin, folded small and tucked away.

This caused a problem between Jean and me, a problem in my second marriage. She did not approve of my rainy-day strategy, thought I was being selfish, proud, perverse in resisting her desires, perverse in deciding for myself without benefit of her counsel. That money did not belong to me, it belonged to us. It should be in the bank earning interest. For a long time I would give her a blank stare when we argued about this. Even during marriage counseling. Especially during marriage counseling.

1999, sometime in the autumn. We went to New York to visit Jean's son, my stepson. We took him and a friend of his out for dinner, in the East Village, near the "alphabets," the streets named A, B, C, and D, the neighborhood of "NYPD Blue." When the bill came, a hundred and sixty dollars, I tried to pay with my American Express card, but the restaurant did not take credit cards. Not even Visa and MasterCard. I reached into my front pocket, where I keep my walking around money. Ninety dollars, three or four twenties, maybe a ten or two, fives and ones. Ninety dollars.

I turned to Jean, but she had no cash. The kids were our guests, and I wasn't about to ask them. So I went back into my wallet and dug out my Benjamin. Now I had a hundred and ninety bucks, just enough for the bill and a decent tip. I was proud. I felt like a hero. My system had saved the day.

A couple of weeks later the subject arose again. Jean and I were discussing our problems, riding in the car, heading north to Carlisle for some reason. I asked her if she had thought again, if maybe she had changed her mind. About the secret Benjamin, about my tucked and folded hundred-dollar bill.

"No," she said. She had not changed her mind. I was still being perverse. Bull-headed, selfish, proud. Maybe I thought I was running my own show, but it was her show too. That was her hundred-dollar bill too. I had no exclusive right to it.

"Like the restaurant bill?" That was my instinctive answer.

She answered me with a huh. She said, "Huh?"

"The restaurant bill, in New York," I said. "Was that yours too?" I was asking her to figure it out.

She figured it out. I could have gone to an ATM. Three, maybe four blocks, five maximum. I did not need to be carrying that money. I could have gone foraging the midnight East Village streets looking for an ATM. It would have been better. It would have shown respect for her, her needs.

"Pride can be fatal to a marriage," she could have said. "Pride carried to the point of perversity." I would have heard her. I would have listened to what she had to say, listened to every word. I would have known she was right.

Lee's Problem

I admire John Doyle Lee, like and admire him, think I understand him. And I feel we are alike in some ways, despite many differences.

Lee was a believer, a true believer. A true and loyal follower. He believed in Joseph and in Joseph's church. He followed Joseph to Joseph's death. He believed in Brigham and in Brigham's version of Joseph's church. He followed Brigham to the end of the earth, to Zion, to the desert, to the valley of the Great Salt Lake. He followed Brigham until he himself was dead. John Doyle Lee followed Brigham Young until Brigham Young killed John Doyle Lee.

Lee's problem was his blind belief, his willingness to follow his leaders blindly. His readiness to kill if he thought his church wanted him to. I do not have that problem, not as my everyday self, certainly not in the guise of the character I call *I*. *I* is defiant, a "lone wolf," what in the West they call an "independent cuss."

I follows himself, sometimes blindly. *I* does what *I* thinks is right. Sometimes *I* is wrong, maybe often, for sure more often than *I* would admit. But *I* will defy anyone. If *I* thinks it is necessary to do so, *I* will defy anyone. Even himself.

Lee's Conversion

John Doyle Lee moved from Kaskaskia north to Vadalia, still in Illinois, where his sister Eliza lived. He married Agatha Woolsey in 1833. In the autumn of 1837 a Mormon missionary, reviled by the local preachers and shunned by the community, knocked on Lee's door and requested a bed for the night.

Lee was sympathetic to the reviled man and took him in, but told him not to preach. Elder King obeyed the restriction, impressed Lee with his sincerity, his humility. In the spring Lee read The Book of Mormon, was converted, moved west to the Mormon settlement in Missouri.

A man of high energy, hard working, intelligent, Lee devoted himself to the church and was rewarded in his turn. In 1843 was the seventh of forty chosen by Joseph to police the new city of Nauvoo. Named by Brigham, after Joseph's death, as member of and secretary to the Council of Fifty. Appointed to keep the temple records. Sealed second of thirty-eight "sons" adopted by Brigham in 1845. All special honors.

In 1847 he was named leader of Summer Quarters, "Brigham's Farm," charged to grow crops for next year's migration to Zion. A tireless worker and ferocious leader, he demanded more of his men than they were willing to give, demanded unquestioning obedience. When challenged, he would not back down.

The men brought a complaint against him. Lee was tried by the church leaders and rebuked for his harshness, but acquitted of wrongdoing. Later Brigham Young said to Lee:

> A few days after your last trial we were in council one night—Wilford, Heber and I, and your name came up. We discussed the trouble with Charlie Kennedy and the other

boys at the farm and all of a sudden—you know how he is—Heber spoke up and said, "Brother Brigham, I want to prophesy."

"Son of Man, Prophesy!" I said.

Well, he started out in a solemn voice, "In the name of Israel's God, this man Lee who now is so much spoken evil of, will yet destroy and trample under his feet, and walk over their graves, those that would destroy him."

Was often the reviled man. Proud, perverse, hard-working, demanding. Resented. Envied. Reviled.

One Man Was Named

1850, Salt Lake City, three years after the Great Migration. John Doyle Lee had built his home, settled his families, and was well on his way to prosperity. Brigham's dream was to colonize southern Utah. He ordered his most capable men, his strongest leaders, Lee among them, to lead the effort. Lee did not want to go, but he would not disobey the prophet, so he went. First to Parowan, Iron County, then on to Harmony, Washington County, in 1854. He served as probate judge, clerk, assessor. He built homes, settled his families, became prosperous.

Then the trouble started. The United States Army was marching on Utah. Emigrants were on the move. Warnings were issued, men called to arms. Brigham's sermons grew increasingly incendiary. He sent General Smith south, to rally the people: "George A. Smith brought the word to the southern settlements, and everywhere he went he spoke in terms of repulsing the approaching army, of defending their homes and firesides, protecting their wives and children against such persecutions as many had suffered before." The enemy was at hand in the guise of the Fancher Party, from Arkansas and Missouri. The enemy was in their midst. Juanita Brooks blames George A. Smith for making the massacre possible, for making it inevitable.

After the massacre came the vow of silence, the agreement to blame the Indians. But soon the rumors started, the whispers. People visited the killing field, saw the bones, the sunbonnets, the scraps of hair hanging from brush.

A series of investigations began almost immediately. In 1858 George A. Smith came south again, not to inflame this time but to look. Of all the people Brigham could have sent to investigate the massacre, he chose one of the most guilty, George A. Smith.

A meeting was held, a first report written and issued. All the major perps attended the meeting, John Doyle Lee among them. This report blamed the Indians. Others may have acted badly, it was said, but the Indians had done the actual killing.

A week later, another meeting was held, another report written and issued. John Doyle Lee was not present at this meeting. The name of Dame came up, Bishop William H. Dame, the man who gave the final order to kill. Smith was presiding, George A. Smith. When Dame was accused, he rose from his chair and declared: "You can NOT lay this onto me! I will not take it! If you dare try, I'll just put the saddle onto the right horse, and you all know well who that is!" Juanita Brooks surely knew: "It could be no other than George A. Smith himself, sitting at the head of the table."

George A. Smith cleared his throat, said it did not seem right to blame Bishop Dame, and everyone agreed. When the report was issued, only one man was named, the one man who had not attended the meeting. Here is what George A. Smith wrote in his report: "John D. Lee and a few other white men were on the ground during a portion of the combat, but for what purpose or how they conducted or whether indeed they were there at all, I have not learned."

Because the Indians were being blamed, Lee was the logical Mormon to name. Juanita Brooks: "If Dame is without guilt, who then was responsible? Who, indeed, except for John D. Lee? As Indian Farmer, he could be held to account for the conduct of the natives, in some degree at least. Not being present, he had no defense."

One Man Stayed Behind

1859. In the spring Judge Cradlebaugh arrived to investigate

George A. Smith

the massacre on behalf of the United States government. Federal Judge Cradlebaugh, from back east, from Washington, D.C., came to interview those most concerned, the men in charge of the south, the perps. None of them could be found. They were hiding in the mountains, in the desert. Later most of them left the area entirely. Lee hid until the judge went back home.

Lee emerged from hiding and resumed his life. Others did not resume: "Almost every man who had been at the Meadows that day took his family or families and left, some north to Cache Valley, some south to Arizona, a few to the desert outposts, but all with the desire of getting so far away that their children would never even hear of the massacre, and would never connect their fathers with it."

Lee did not go. Lee stayed. He tilled his land, he ran his businesses, he tended to the welfare of his families. Lee had wives. Lee had sons and daughters. Lee had houses in Washington and Harmony.

Lee remained a player in his communities, was a big shot, a preacher, a player, one of the richest men in town, both towns. When Brigham came south, he stayed with John Doyle Lee, Brigham and his train, his entourage. All of them stayed in John Doyle Lee's houses and ate his food. In this way was Lee honored by his leader. Everything seemed all right.

Part VIII
Comes the Law

The Best Days Are the First to Flee

1859, 1860, and 1861. The most prosperous years in the life of John Doyle Lee, the best years and days, the years of success and high standing. Houses in Harmony and Washington in southern Utah, houses "well stocked with cured meats, cheese, crocks of butter, sacks of dried fruit, and pits of carrots and potatoes." Thirty fifty-gallon barrels of molasses, whole clingstone peaches cooked in molasses syrup and put up in sealed crocks.

He started building a new house in Washington, a larger house, a stone mansion. "Carpenters were putting in doors and windows, floors and ceilings, and building mantels, cupboards, and closets. Stone masons were putting up a large stone granary behind the house, and when it was finished built an outhouse with a shingle roof. One evidence of a family's status was the quality of toilet facilities it provided, and Lee wanted his to be of the best." Juanita Brooks.

Giving of his time to the community, his labor, his ideas, his wealth. Attending church regularly and preaching often. Healing the sick and injured, perhaps his greatest gift. The Mormons believed in the laying on of hands for spiritual healing, and Lee was one of the best. In 1860, January, the eighteenth, Lee wrote in his diary (quoted errors and all):

> About 10 m. a shocking occurrence happened. Wm. Slade shot from one of my doors at a crow. The ball glanced &

struck one of Br. Wm. Wood litle girls above the fore head, Shot away the Scull, leaving the Brain Pan bare. The alarm was given, the Neighbors flocked to the Scene. The child lay in its gore, apparently lifeless, the Parrents almost frantic. I called them to order, laid hands on it, with Elder Freem & others, rebuked the Powers of Death, & asked the Lord to raise it, & the child immediately came too. This gave confidence to all presant, & I hope it will be a warning to all carless shooting.

A typical case, except for the gunplay. John Doyle Lee, known to all, and in great demand, for his power of healing. Once healed a horse by the laying on of hands.

1859, 1860, 1861, the best years for John Doyle Lee. 1857, the Mountain Meadows Massacre, the cover-up, the oaths of secrecy. Then the investigations, the reports, one man singled out in the second report. John Doyle Lee, the only one of the perps who stayed behind when things got tough. The search was well under way. The search for a scapegoat, for someone to blame. John Doyle Lee was down south, tending to business, unaware.

Massacre at the Pond House

2003. Early in the year, perhaps February. A family incident at the Pond House, our old farmhouse. Melanie misbehaved. She wrote messages on the Internet, messages to strangers, messages written on Sheila's account and signed with Sheila's name. Messages with a picture labeled, "This is me." A picture that was not "me," not Melanie, not Sheila. A semi-racy picture, a kind of invitation. Sheila found out. The time had come for talk.

Sheila talked. Melanie proclaimed her innocence. Sheila said, "My foot." Sheila said, "Innocent, my foot." Sheila raised her voice. Melanie yelled back.

I was upstairs. I and *I* were upstairs, maybe in my home office, writing about the Mormons, maybe in the bedroom, unbuttoning a month's worth of shirts, getting them ready for the laundry.

I heard the yelling. I heard Sheila yell, "Do you know the people you are writing to? Do you know what kind of people are out there?"

I came downstairs. I said, "Melanie, did you do this?"

Melanie said, "Leave me alone," and headed for the door.

Sheila yelled, "Get back here." Melanie ran upstairs. I followed, a little too excited, close behind her. *I* was getting involved. *I* chased her up the stairs.

Melanie went into the bathroom. She was pushing the door shut, trying to lock it. *I* made his mistake.

I pushed the door against her, pushed it open. Melanie fell into the tub. *I* pulled her out, pulled her into the hallway, tried to get her back downstairs. She resisted. *I* grabbed her, one hand landed on her neck. She pulled away. *I* scratched her neck. *I* left an ugly scratch upon her neck.

I should have stayed in control, sat down on the stairs outside the bathroom. I should have calmed down and waited. But I let *I* take over, and *I* pushed open the door, *I* pulled her out, *I* scratched her neck. Only then did *I* let go.

Gossip Is Not Gospel

A just man and fair, John Doyle Lee. Gave no honor to gossip. Wanted the facts, both sides of the story, this story. Young Nephi Stewart came to Washington from the town of Beaver. Rumors followed him, gossipy accusations. He was a stealer of horses, he had deserted his wife. The bishop at Washington was outraged and recommended shunning, said the hand of fellowship must be withdrawn from Nephi Stewart. No one was to invite him home for dinner, no one was to talk to him, no one was to give him a job.

John Doyle Lee wrote his disagreement in his diary: "Reports says that [Stewart] is a bad man. But I am not authorised to believe & credit all reports, especially where the character & Life of a man is at stake. I would certainly be unwise to Judge a Mater [sic] [without] hearing both sides & investigating it carefully."

Lee investigated. He sat down with the sinner, asked questions, listened to answers, decided that Stewart "had been dealt with unjustly."

The bishop disagreed, maintained his outrage, held his ground, hardened his stand. According to Lee's diary, the bishop said that Stewart "ought to be drove out from us to the Piutes Indians on the Muddy & he would be one to help doo it, & if any man wanted to Shoot him, to Shoot & be Damned."

A meeting was held. The bishop was there, John Doyle Lee was there, Collins was there, a man identified as Collins, the second counselor of the ward, the Mormon ward in Washington. Collins spoke. He had recently come from Beaver and claimed firsthand knowledge of Stewart. Collins said Stewart was an honest young man. A good fiddler, a good singer, a worthy companion. The bishop remained outraged.

John Doyle Lee had a solution. He would hire Stewart to work on his land. He would keep him away from the bishop. Stewart worked for Lee for many years, caused no trouble, deserted no wives, stole no horses. He proved himself to be a good fiddler, a worthy companion, an honest young man. The gossip was wrong. Nephi Stewart was a good man.

The Police Are Coming

Melanie ran. After *I* pushed open the door and knocked her down. After *I* pulled her out of the bathroom and scratched her neck. Melanie ran down the stairs and out the front door, into the winter night. I did not chase her. I knew I had done enough. I knew *I* had done too much. I watched her leave from the top of the stairs.

We conferred, Sheila and I, wondered where she had gone. We went outside and walked around the house. We asked her younger sisters. Where did they think she went? They said maybe behind the barn. We looked behind the barn. I went out and looked in the woods. A briar tore a hole in my new leather jacket.

We calmed her younger sisters, asked them if they were all right. I asked them if they would help me look for Melanie. The three of us, the girls and I, drove to Megan's house, Melanie's best friend, Megan the Vegan. The girls knocked on the door, but no one answered. They could see Megan's mother inside, but Megan's mother did not come to the door.

Sheila was working the phone. She called Barb, who lives next door. Barb had not seen Melanie. Her daughters had not seen Melanie either. They said they would look for her.

Sheila called Megan's house. Megan's mom answered. "Yes," said Megan's mom, "Melanie is here."

"Thank God," said Sheila. "Let me talk to her."

"No," said Megan's mom. "You cannot talk to her. The police are coming."

The Gradual Shunning of John Doyle Lee

The gossip persisted. The gossip continued and grew, focused now entirely on John Doyle Lee, the only man to stay behind, the only participant in the massacre who did not flee, to the mountains, to the desert, to Arizona or Nevada. The shunning began, the gradual shunning of John Doyle Lee.

In 1859 he was replaced as probate judge. Lee made nothing of it, "but"—Juanita Brooks—"his association with the massacre was without doubt the reason for his dismissal."

His reputation continued to decline. In 1864, a group of parishioners suggested that he resign as bishop of Harmony Ward, and he did so. By 1866 he was generally suspected and disliked by the people at Harmony. Juanita Brooks says this happened "in spite of everything." Despite Lee's wealth. Despite his service to his church, to his community, to his people. Despite his gift of healing.

Or perhaps because of these things, because of his general success. "Perhaps his very industry, his driving use of his family and hired help, his shrewd trading, his ability to amass property and to live well made his neighbors all the more critical of him."

The whispering continued, the whispering about the massacre and John Doyle Lee. The stories were many and colorful, and the

Mormons hated what they heard. Massacre was not a Mormon thing to do, not a Christian thing.

In 1870, in February, Brigham Young felt the need to protect the church. He came south to counsel John Doyle Lee. He told him he should move, flee, go live in the desert or the mountains, in Arizona or Nevada. Lee stayed.

Brigham returned in September to speak again with Lee:

> "I should like to see you enjoy peace for your remaining years," the president said. "Gather your wives and children around you, select some fertile valley, and settle."
>
> Lee hesitated. "Well, if it is your wish and counsel..."
>
> "It is my wish and counsel." The voice was firm to sharpness.... Lee knew that his future was set.

He began his move. East, into wilder country, to Panguitch, then south of Panguitch to Kanab.

The Rules of Adoption

Melanie is an adopted child. Before being adopted she was a foster child. She is smart, and she knows the rules, the rules of foster parenting, the rules of pre-adoption. The rules governing discipline. The child shall not be touched. Would-be parents must be tested under pressure, must prove themselves. Discipline that involves physical contact, including restraint, may be abuse. The child may be taken away.

The law is different now that Melanie is fully adopted. But she remembers those earlier rules.

In her heart Melanie knew she had been abused. Melanie explained it all to Megan and Megan's mother, the mother who forbids dancing, Halloween, birthdays, and gifts at Christmas. The mother who forbade Melanie to come to her house, after the one time, three years ago, when Melanie was too loud.

Melanie explained the massacre to Megan's mother. The mother of our "fourth daughter," who all but lived with us for three years, the mother who does hair and has Jesus in her heart. Melanie told her story to Megan's mother, and Megan's mother called the police.

A state trooper arrived at Megan's house. He talked to Melanie. He came to the Pond House. He talked to Sheila, he talked to me. He talked to each of us alone. He talked to us together. He talked to Melanie's sisters.

He said, "Melanie is upset, but she is fine." He said he understood the situation, he sees it every day, the struggle for control. He did not see evidence of abuse, no need for further action. He said, "This seems bad, I know, but wait until she is fourteen."

Excommunication

Lee had moved away, but events were moving faster, faster than John Doyle Lee was moving. The pressures on Brigham had become irresistible.

October, 1870, the eighth. Lee was excommunicated by the Church of Jesus Christ of Latter-day Saints, Lee's church. Excommunicated by Brigham Young, Lee's adoptive father. John Doyle Lee was excommunicated from the Mormon church by the man he thought was next in line to God.

Lee wished to appeal, wanted to be understood. He tried to meet with Brigham, but Brigham sent him to Bishop Snow. Lee talked with Snow, and Snow talked with Brigham Young. Brigham told Bishop Snow to write a letter "To J. D. Lee at Washington":

> If you will consult your own safety & that of others, you will not press yourself nor an investigation on others at this time least [sic] you cause others to become accessory with you & thereby force them to inform upon you or to suffer. Our advice is, Trust no one. Make yourself scarce & keep out of the way.

The excommunication was not rescinded. The leaders did not wish to martyr Lee, or so they said. Nor did they suggest that he trust them. His presence was a problem, a reminder of the massacre, an embarrassment to the church. John Doyle Lee was a lightning rod for the rumors, adding fuel to the blazing gossip. The bishop and the prophet told him to do the right thing, to go away. Get far away from the church, far away from the bishops and the prophets.

Lee moved farther south, farther from civilization. To a ferry on the Colorado River, just over the border into Arizona, the place now known as Lee's Ferry. To "land which for the next years was to be his greatest threat and antagonist." To a place so hot in summer, it "was no fit habitat for man or beast." A place "of endless stretches of barrenness in various tones of red, an area of hogbacks dotted with sparse, scraggly brush with writhing gullies between them."

When Lee's wife Emma saw the place, she named it Lonely Dell.

Emma came south, and Rachel, another wife, and several children of all ages. Many wives and children stayed behind. In Harmony, in Washington, in Kanab and Panguitch. Lee made annual visits, trips back and forth, forth and back. Gathering supplies, seeing to business, checking on his families.

The Family Meeting

The school called. Melanie had gone to the nurse, about the scratch on her neck, about the massacre at the Pond House. The school was required to file a report to Children's Services, and the county got involved. A second nurse examined the neck. A social worker came to the house. She interviewed the family. She heard the versions, talked to both nurses, filed her own report.

The injury was superficial, an ugly mark on the skin. Not proof of abuse. But the county saw a lack of order, a lack of proper control, a need for discipline. A need for family therapy.

Mark came, Mark the county therapist. Once a week for twelve weeks, one hour per week. One hour one night per week for twelve weeks. Everybody talked. We all endured the family therapy.

Mark encouraged family meetings, another kind of therapy, a continuation of the family therapy. We held a family meeting, asked the kids their thoughts. Melanie spoke first, justified her actions,

Chuckie Walker Peeling Corn

proclaimed her innocence and her martyrdom. Saint Melanie of the bathroom and the stair.

Crystal snorted. "You know that's not right, Melanie," she said. "You caused the whole thing. You got into mom's computer. You wrote the e-mails."

Rebekkah snorted too. Both of the younger kids were calm. Rebekkah said, "Yeah, Melanie. Peter didn't hurt you. You hurt the whole family. You ran to Megan's house. You ran to Megan's mom. You lied about the family."

Melanie responded with silence, Melanie struck dumb by her sisters.

A Hung Jury

The investigations continued. The inquiries spread. Eventually warrants were issued. In 1874 warrants for the apprehension of eight men suspected of participating in the massacre were issued. Sheriff William Stokes of Beaver was in charge: "Because most of these men were out of the state, either in Arizona or Nevada, and since Lee was known to make annual visits in to the settlements, Stokes decided to get him first, even if he had to follow him all the way to the river."

November, the seventh. Lee was arrested in Panguitch, and Stokes stopped searching. He had his man. Using this man he could flush out the others, by making Lee testify, by making him break the vow of silence.

A trial was set for July of 1875, eight months hence. Lee would spend that time under guard, eight months and thirteen days. Stokes wrote that Lee remained cheerful and cooperative, and "never gave any trouble to me or his guards. He never tried to escape, but at all times assisted his guards to carry out the instructions they had received from the officers."

At the end of the trial, the jury could not agree. Eight Mormons voted for acquittal, four gentiles voted for conviction. Philip Klingensmith had testified, a participant in the massacre and the only eyewitness to appear at the trial. "He made it very clear that Isaac C. Haight had said that 'he had orders from headquarters to kill all of the said company of emigrants except the little children,' but did not know whether said orders came from the regimental headquarters at Parowan or from the commander in chief at Salt Lake City." The commander in chief: Brigham Young, President Brigham Young of the Church of Jesus Christ of Latter-day Saints.

Klingensmith told the truth as he knew it. He was not near Lee on the killing field, and he did not know what Lee did there. He did know these three things, and I quote from the summary of his testimony:

1. Lee was not at the council meeting, so had no part in initiating the idea.
2. After the first [Indian] attack, Lee tried to call off the massacre; that he did all he could to stop it.
3. Lee received orders to decoy the emigrants out and disarm them, from Higbee, who carried them from Haight, who in turn got them from Dame.

The trial ended with a hung jury. In 1875, on the fifth of August. Eight Mormon jurors voted for acquittal, and four gentiles voted for conviction. A second trial would be necessary.

The Truth about Peter

2003, over the summer. Words were spoken in the beauty parlor. Above the scissors and the comb. Over the sound of the hair dryer. Words spoken by the beautician with Jesus in her heart. Knowing looks were exchanged in the mirror. The truth was getting out. The gospel was being preached. To the women, the other mothers in the neighborhood. First the old news: a dance, a plot, a cover-up, a series of lies. Now this: a beating, an attempted strangulation, an innocent girl thrown down the stairs.

Autumn, 2003, sometime in October. The phone rang at the Pond House. A neighbor was calling, another mother calling Sheila, from a house down the road. "Oh God," said Sheila when she heard who was calling, "not her again."

Two years earlier Sheila had called her, about the woman's dogs tipping over our garbage cans, spreading the stuff around. The woman explained that her dogs were just dogs. Dogs could not be blamed if people were dumb enough to put food scraps in their garbage cans. Sheila explained the township rule that dogs be confined to the yards of their owners. The dog continued its raids.

Another the time the woman and her husband and their two daughters came to complain that their youngest son was being teased by Melanie on the bus. They spoke to me. I was to discipline Melanie, knock some sense into her head. Instead I called Melanie down from upstairs, asked for her version. "Well, I never!" said the woman.

Then just this year, a few months ago. Melanie and the older son were talking on the phone, exchanging notes at school, maybe some kind of puppy love. But the girl was brown, and the boy was lily white. The end of Western civilization was at hand.

Now she was calling about the money. Melanie had taken forty dollars from my wallet and given it to the boy. We knew this, we talked about it with Mark, the therapist from the county. Mark said that kids will do that, insecure kids, adopted kids whose parents then divorced, kids who were moved across the country, kids with a new stepdad. Kids like that might steal from their parents and try to buy affection from their friends. One solution was to hide my wallet.

At first the woman seemed almost calm. "We don't have to hide our money," she said. "And I know the problem isn't Melanie. Melanie is probably a good kid. She can come over and play any time." The offer was bizarre for kids that age. Sheila felt uneasy.

The woman said, "I heard about the fight. I know what's going on."

"What?" Sheila was anxious now. "What's going on?"

"Come on," the woman said. "You don't have to pretend with me. I have talked to the neighbors. I know the truth."

"What?" said Sheila. "What are you talking about?"

"I am talking about your husband. I am talking about Peter. Peter is the problem. Everyone says he is a monster." The woman had heard the gossip, maybe at the beauty parlor. Now she was preaching the truth, spreading the gospel.

Baseball at the Pond House

March, 2004, late in the month. The snow is gone. The rains have come. The ground behind the barn is mostly mud. Water stands in puddles.

"Peter, take me to Wal-Mart. Peter, buy me a glove."

"Jesus, Melanie. Can't you wait even a minute? I have work to do. I have a life of my own."

"Yeah," she drawls. "Rrrr-ight. *You* have a life."

The gloves are on sale. But what about a bat? And "Peter, can we get one of these balls?" Nice white ones, shrink-wrapped in cellophane.

A few days later, we are out behind the barn playing catch. Melanie has a good arm, a funny hitch as she throws. I admire the swallows, cruising for insects.

Melanie says, "Don't throw it right to me. Give me some pop-ups. Make me run." I throw pop-ups, lead her toward the puddles, have a little fun.

Evening sneaking in. I see a bat, the furry kind, fluttering past a tree. "Hey Melanie," I say, "look at the…*Ooof!*" The ball hits me in the belly. Melanie did not notice me looking away. She was throwing out the runner at home. It could have been worse.

Two weeks later it is worse. Melanie is at the plate, batting. I am standing fifteen or twenty feet away, pitching baseballs underhand, hard balls. Melanie hits a line drive straight at me. I turn just in time, take it on the thigh. High on the inner thigh. Melanie giggles…frowns…asks, "Are you all right?"

"Yeah, I'm fine," I hiss, gritting my teeth.

We are doing our thing. Playing our game. Cooking our gooses. I am cooking Melanie's goose. Melanie is cooking mine. Melanie is cooking Melanie's goose. I am cooking mine.

Part IX
Expediency and Sin

The Best Guard

1875. John Doyle Lee was arrested and put on trial for the Mountain Meadows Massacre. The only one of fifty perps to be charged, the only one to face the music. On the eighth of August, the trial ended without a verdict. The jurors split along religious lines, eight Mormons voting for acquittal, four gentiles voting for conviction. A second trial was scheduled.

Time to kill awaiting the second trial. Lee was marched north to the Utah State Penitentiary in Salt Lake City, escorted by two guards under the command of George R. Maxwell, US marshal. The two men hit it off. Lee liked Maxwell, and Maxwell liked Lee. Lee liked Maxwell enough to give him an affectionate nickname. He called his captor "the general," General Maxwell.

The trip took three days, two nights. The party, Lee, Maxwell, and the guards, spent the first night in the mountains. Even in August the night air was cold for sleeping. Lee shared a tent with General Maxwell, but arose before daylight, collected a pile of wood and started a fire. In his diary Lee described what happened when he woke Maxwell: "The General looking around seeing the guard all asleep, turned to me with a smile and said, 'I believe you are the best guard that I have.'"

John Doyle Lee standing guard over himself, in the night, on his way to prison, the only perp arrested for the crime, the only one who did not run.

Pulling the Weeds

April, 2003, the twenty-ninth, evening, daylight-saving time, still bright. Crystal is on her knees in front of the Pond House, preparing the flower beds. The middle daughter, the second of three half sisters, one birth mother, three birth fathers, two of them unknown. Then an adoptive father, then me, the stepfather.

We hit it off right away, and we get along just fine. She likes me, and I like her. I like her well enough to have given her a nickname, an affectionate nickname. I call her Crystalline Crystal. She is clear as sunshine, a jewel, facets and depths. She loves everything natural, everything outdoors. She gazes at it long and long. She brings me insects, small animals, snakes, creatures dug from the earth. Huge spiders crawling over her hands. She grabs them without hesitation and has no fear, never has had any. Born that way, I guess. Go figure.

Now she is working on the flower beds in the front yard of the Pond House. She has been out there for hours, working with dedication, concentration, staying power. Pulling weeds, raking leaves, loosening the soil. I cannot do it the way she does. I get tired, bored. She sticks with it. Halfway done now, one side all cleared out, spaded.

I was just downstairs, watching her. From inside the front door, myself unseen. She was squatting over the cleared earth, peering. At what? Something crawling? She picked it up, studied it, put it back, picked up something else, studied, cast it aside. Got up, went to the other side, began pulling at the weeds.

I roused myself, returned to my home office, walked back upstairs to write some prose. Today is Tuesday, a beautiful evening, finally. Rain in the morning, then sun by evening, a beautiful time of day. The best of springtime.

Learning to Read and Write

The State Penitentiary was at Sugarhouse, in the part of Salt Lake City still known today as Sugarhouse. The prison was a terrible place. The prisoners slept on boards, were badly fed, fought one another often. Malefactors were chained in the Iron Cage. Swarming bedbugs were the least of anyone's worries.

John Doyle Lee was the only devout Mormon in the yard, the only educated man. Another prisoner, a young man named Phelps, asked Lee to teach him to read, so Lee started a school. Built the tables and benches himself by hand. Held classes every day, including Sunday.

The *Salt Lake Tribune* noticed. In its "Penitentiary Notes," the *Salt Lake Tribune* reported: "John D. Lee's free school is progressing nicely & a number of the prisoners are rapidly learning to read & write. Lee is ahead of his old pal Brigham on the free school question at least, and is as good a man in other respects;—the only difference being that one is in jail & the other ought to be." The *Tribune* is the independent paper, even today. The *Deseret News* speaks for the Mormons.

Lee was still devoted to Brigham. One of Brigham's sealed and adopted sons. The real betrayal was yet to come.

Planting the Trees

Last Sunday we transplanted trees. The twenty-seventh of April, 2003, two days ago, five of them, silver maples. Seeds had landed in the pond and sprouted, a year, two years, ago. I dug five of them out of the muck, the silt, their roots dripping water. Crystal was with me, Crystalline Crystal. She watched me dig up the trees. She wanted to help.

We put the trees into the cart that attaches to the tractor, the garden tractor, stopped off at the shed and picked up the shovel, some fertilizer, some four-foot stakes, some rope, the hatchet. We drove to the first spot, on the lawn near the road, the field on the west side of the house. The field the farmer used to cut for hay.

I had barely started cutting the turf when Crystal said, "Let me. I want to do it," she said.

I gave up the shovel, agreed to let her try, but first I warned her. "This job is hard," I said. "Hard and frustrating. Cutting through the turf then fighting with the rocks and shale. It is not fun. It's hard, frustrating work."

"I want to do it," she said. She did it. She dug the hole exactly as I would have done it. She set the shovel aside. We started to plant the first tree.

Trust No One

John Doyle Lee spent another eighteen months in prison, waiting for his second trial, teaching school, writing in his journal. Thinking about the present and meditating on his past.

Visitors came, his friend the US marshal, George R. Maxwell, the general. Sheriff Stokes, his other friend. Officers, agents of the court, gentiles, men who had arrested and escorted the prisoner. Men who had taken the measure of John Doyle Lee.

They offered him a deal. Tell the truth and walk. Name the names, describe the deeds, link the names with the deeds. Give up your former friends. Just tell the truth and you can go. Home to your wives and children. Home today.

Lee refused to talk. He had taken a vow of silence. Standing on the killing field in the morning, the morning after the massacre, all the men had vowed their silence on pain of death. For mutual self-protection, to shield the church from shame. The Indians had done the killing. There was no one here but us Indians. The officers implored him to talk, but Lee stayed silent.

Others talked. Once the trial started, the second trial, others began to talk. About John Doyle Lee. They came down from the mountains, came out of the desert, traveled back from Arizona and Nevada, to testify at the second trial of John Doyle Lee. Juanita Brooks: "If one is to trust verbal reports, these men were ordered to appear by Brigham Young." Would they have come otherwise? When pigs take off and fly.

Juanita Brooks was born in southern Utah, in Saint George, near Washington, not far from Harmony, Cedar City, the killing fields at Mountain Meadows. A lifelong Mormon. As a child she heard

Juanita Brooks

the stories about the massacre, about that monster John Doyle Lee.

Juanita Brooks grew up, went to school, earned a doctorate, became a professor of English. She looked into the rumors. She interviewed the old timers. She discovered the cover-up, learned the truth about John Doyle Lee, figured out the scapegoating, wrote the book, the books. *The Mountain Meadows Massacre* and *John Doyle Lee*, the life of John Doyle Lee.

The letters were never found. The letters from Brigham ordering the men to appear, said to have been written but never found. If one is to believe the old-timers, letters were written and sent, received and read, understood and acted upon. Nephi Johnson's daughter "had seen the letter advising him, [but] did not have it in her possession[,] nor did she know where it could be found. The family of Jacob Hamblin said that he received a similar letter from Brigham Young, but again the actual letter is not available."

They must have been burned. In all probability, the letters were burned. "Trust no one." Destroy this letter. Do as you are told.

The Walker Clan

Rebekkah appeared just as we were starting to plant the first tree. Rebekkah, the youngest child, the one I call Chuckie Walker, the youngest member of the Walker clan. We call ourselves the Walker clan. In the words of Sheila, we are *The Whole Dern Walker Clan*. So named in honor of Leadbelly, Huddie Leadbetter, in honor of his song:

> Little Sally Walker
> Sitting in the saucer
> Weeping and a-moaning
> Like a turtle dove.
>
> Rise Sally rise,
> Wipe your weeping eyes,
> Fly to the east, fly to the west,
> Fly to the one that you love the best.

A repetitive children's song. These verses are repeated, over and over, each time with a different name. A different first name, but always they are Walkers. "It has to be Walker," Leadbelly explains in the middle of the song, "so it'll rhyme with saucer."

The girls love the song. Sheila and I love the song. The five of us sing along with Leadbelly while riding in the car. The adoptive mother, the stepfather, the three half sisters, The Whole Dern Walker Clan.

Because of the song, I started to call Rebekkah Chuckie Walker. Chuckie Walker is my current affectionate nickname for the youngest girl, Rebekkah. Before I started to call her Chuckie Walker, I called her Chuckie, and before I called her Chuckie, I called her Rebekkah. Just plain Rebekkah.

The One-Act Play

The trial proceeded as though by script. Juanita Brooks: "Even the most cursory examination of the court records will show that between the first and second trials of Lee, something happened." A script was all but written, a one-act play with seven scenes. The action was planned, the plot laid down, the verdict already known. Probably by Brigham, Brigham and his minions.

A one-act play designed to star and be directed by District Attorney Sumner Howard. Seven lesser roles, played by the returning perps. A jury of twelve Mormons, ordered to vote "guilty," for the good of the church, to put the scandal to rest, to bury it with the body of the defendant, the scapegoat, the sacrificial lamb. The scandal of the massacre was to be buried with the body of John Doyle Lee.

Daniel H. Wells was the first of the seven witnesses. At the time of the massacre, Wells was the leader of the Nauvoo Legion, the Mormon militia. When asked about Lee's standing in the legion at the time, Wells answered: "[Lee] had been a major in the military. I don't remember whether he was [then] or not. At that particular time, I think not. I think he had been superseded." Juanita Brooks:

"This testimony seemed inoffensive enough, but it removed Lee from authority in the military, so that whatever he did was without orders from or sanction by them."

Laban Morrill had attended the meeting on massacre eve, the meeting at which the killing was planned, the meeting from which Lee was absent. Morrill claimed the group was indecisive, afraid to act, and so they decided to stall. One rider would be sent to Brigham, asking for advice. Another rider would be sent to Lee, ordering him to control the Indians. "Here again was a short, effective testimony, with only one point established: that Lee was to hold the Indians in check until word arrived from Brigham Young." The Indians were not held in check, the Mormons were not held in check, the immigrants were dead many days before any rider could return from Salt Lake City.

Joel White, the third witness, was the rider sent to Lee. When told the Indians must be restrained, Lee answered, according to White, "'I don't know about that,' or 'I'll have something to say about that,' or words to that effect." Juanita Brooks: "This would be used to prove that Lee had acted in opposition to the wishes of the local military."

Samuel Knight drove one of the wagons, the one containing the injured immigrants. Lee was with those wagons during the massacre. The injured were to be killed by Lee, by the drivers, by a couple of other Mormons. Lee claimed his gun misfired, said he killed no one. Knight said "his team was so fractious that he could not be positive what did go on..., but it was his impression that John D. Lee had killed...one woman." The trial had been scripted. The evidence did not need to be strong.

Samuel McMurdy, the fifth witness, drove the other wagon, the wagon containing the immigrant children. He said he saw Lee "draw a gun and shoot, and saw a woman fall..., but he too was busy with his horses and did not want to see anything." When asked if he himself had killed anyone, McMurdy replied, "I believe I am not on trial, sir." Juanita Brooks: "The attorneys seemed not to press any point to the embarrassment of a witness, so long as he would testify that John D. Lee had killed at least one person."

Nephi Johnson was not there, at the massacre. Well, he was there, but he watched from a hill, far away. No, not so far away that he could not see. At least he could see the actions of John Doyle Lee, perhaps using spiritual sight. He said he saw Lee shoot a woman, saw him cut a man's throat. "Strangely, he did not see anybody else do anything." Not an Indian, not a Mormon, not an immigrant, not a horse or cow, not a bird in the sky.

Jacob Hamblin "had not been present at the massacre at all and so had no oath of secrecy to keep." He was the last witness, the seventh. He was not present at the massacre, but later ran into John Doyle Lee. He said that Lee had told him this story: an Indian chief found two immigrant women "who had hidden in the brush and escaped the first massacre." The Indian brought the women to Lee, "and he asked him what he should do with them, and the Indian killed one and [Lee] killed the other."

Wanting to hear more about this incident, Sumner Howard invited Hamblin to embellish his story. Hamblin said, "Yes, the women were beautiful. Yes, they were young." No doubt they were mothers, probably pregnant again, perhaps still suckling their recent babes. Guardian angels probably fluttered overhead, no doubt weeping and begging for the lives of these innocent women, who were cut down in cold blood by John Doyle Lee and an Indian chief.

Juanita Brooks:

> By the time the lawyers were through with Jacob Hamblin, the audience was in such a state of horror and shock, they were ready to believe the worst....
>
> So carefully had the questions been placed; so patient and delicate had the lawyers been with the witnesses, that the combined sins of all the fifty men who were present were laid on the shoulders of John D. Lee. By the time the arguments were finished he had been made responsible for planning and executing the murder, in defiance of his

superior officers and contrary to their orders.

The oddest aspect of the trial is this: "Through it all Lee sat facing the court in silence. He called no witnesses; made no defense." No cross-examinations were conducted. John Doyle Lee, devout to the end, helping the church lead him to slaughter.

The result was predictable, quick, and unanimous: "After an hour's consultation the jury brought in a verdict: 'Guilty of murder in the first degree.'" John Doyle Lee was sentenced to death.

Chuckie

2000, two and a half years ago. September? October? Sometime in the fall. I came home from work, said hi to Sheila, saw Rebekkah standing in the doorway between the kitchen and the dining room. She was seven years old.

I greeted her playfully, fooling around. "Who is this little girl?" I asked. "Who is this sweet little thing?"

"My name is Chuckie," Rebekkah said. She said her name was Chuckie.

She had been watching *Rugrats* on TV. She had formed a spiritual bond with Chucky, the *Rugrats* character named Chucky. After that I called her Chuckie, for maybe a year, changing the spelling to distinguish her from the other Chucky, the evil one. Later we listened to the Leadbelly song, so now I call her Chuckie Walker. She is the youngest member of The Whole Dern Walker Clan.

Him

When asked how he wanted to die, Lee replied: "I prefer to be shot." He could have been hanged, but asked that they spill his blood, because of the doctrine of blood atonement. Lee knew that he had sinned. Whether he had killed anyone that day or not, he knew that he had sinned.

The choice of how to be killed had been made for him thirty-nine years earlier, back in Missouri, when Lee was elevated to the group of seventy, the priestly inner council of the Church of Jesus Christ of Latter-day Saints. That is when Lee was given the patriarchal blessing: "Thou shalt come forth in the morning of the first resurrection, and no power shall hinder except the shedding of innocent blood, or consenting thereto." By his presence and his actions at the massacre, Lee had consented to the shedding of innocent blood. Against his will, perhaps, but he had consented.

He knew his own blood must be spilled, the only way he could "atone for the violation of this one condition which would endanger his status in the hereafter." He had to follow the doctrine of blood atonement.

1877, the twenty-third of March. Lee was taken to Mountain Meadows, to be executed on the killing field where the great crime had been committed. Juanita Brooks:

> He shook hands with all those around him, bidding each farewell, took off his overcoat, muffler, and hat to give to friends. His eyes were bound, but at his request, his hands remained free. The minister who had accompanied him knelt on the ground and uttered a short, earnest prayer, to which Lee listened attentively.
>
> As he sat posed on the coffin,...the condemned man said again, "Center my heart, boys. Don't mangle my body!"
>
> At the signal "Ready! Aim! Fire!" five shots rang out, and John D. Lee fell back into his coffin without a moan or a tremor of the body except for a convulsive twitching of the fingers of his left hand.

On the night before his death, Lee wrote a final statement: "I have been treacherously betrayed and sacrificed in the most cowardly manner by those who should have been my friends, and whose will I have diligently striven to make my pleasure for the last thirty years at least. In return for my faithfulness and fidelity to him and his cause, he has sacrificed me in a most shameful and cruel way."

The word strikes the reader like a bullet from a rifle. *Him.* A singular pronoun with a compound and irrelevant antecedent: "those who should have been my friends." The statement refers to Brigham Young. And to Brigham's minions, to be sure. But to Brigham in particular and for sure.

Pouring the Water

Rebekkah walked up to Crystal and me as we were planting the first tree. Chuckie Walker. She wanted to help. She said, "What can I do?"

"We need water," I said. "Use your wagon and the bucket. Put the bucket in the wagon, fill the bucket with water and pull it over here."

We finished planting the first tree. I drove in a stake and tied up the tree while Crystal sprinkled fertilizer. Rebekkah arrived, pulling her wagon, poured the water around the tree.

I watched as Crystal dug the second hole by herself. Then I planted the second tree. Rebekkah went for more water. Crystal was ready to dig the third hole. I laid out holes three through five and distributed the rest of the stakes. I placed the trees beside where the holes would be.

I told Crystal to look at the roots, to shape the holes according to the roots. She dug three more holes, five holes in all, five holes in heavy turf and broken shale, perfect holes. She dug them all. Eleven years old, tenacious, committed, dedicated, a horticulturist, a gardener, an arborist, an ichthyologist. A tenacious, committed, dedicated, hard-working, butt-kicking, nature-loving Crystalline Crystal of a dynamite little girl.

The Button Clerk

Brigham was a button clerk. Joseph Smith was a poet, a creator, a seer, a tortured man inside and out, from within and from without. Joseph was a tortured poet. Brigham was a button clerk.

Brigham had one revelation. Fifty-five wives and one revelation, fifty-seven children and one revelation, thirty-three years as president of the church and one revelation. One conversation with God. Joseph had hundreds of revelations, hundreds of conversations with God. Joseph spoke his revelations in the voice of God, in the voice of thunder,

thunder echoing away to wisdom. To something sounding like wisdom. Sometimes devious and conniving, but sounding like wisdom.

Brigham had one revelation, an organizational revelation. Before the migration, Brigham claimed that God had told him how to organize the people, how to group them. Something about little groups of ten people each, medium groups of five little groups, then the whole group. Each group was to have a leader, and the leaders were to get bigger with the groups. Brigham would be the biggest leader, the autocrat. God revealed all this to Brigham, and Brigham revealed it to the people. Wallace Stegner:

> And when the organizational outline was completed the revelation closed with as clipped a phrase as if God were a business man dictating to his secretary. "And so no more at this time," God said. There was no more at any time. The secretary had taken over the administration of the business.

The revelation was useful, expedient. The emigrants had to be organized, and Brigham wanted no argument. If the plan came from God, there would be no argument. The plan came from God, Brigham's expedient God, and there was no argument.

Brigham was a secretary. Autocratic, expeditious, but a secretary. A button clerk. A button clerk with fifty-five wives, fifty-seven children, and the power of blood atonement, the power of Vito Corleone.

The Amazing Crystalline Crystal

September 2003. The trees are still alive, the five trees transplanted in April from the pond. In the holes dug by Crystal. Those five trees are still alive, transplanted silver maples, as close to worthless as a maple tree can get.

There was another maple, a hard maple, from down in the woods. I transplanted that one myself to be certain it was done right, also in April. I thought of it as my prize tree. It started to die sometime in July. The summer was unusually wet, but the tree started to die in July. I could not save it. Nothing I tried could save that tree.

Crystalline Crystal

I also planted ten dogwoods that I purchased in bulk from the county extension service. The trees were not guaranteed, but three leaves eventually appeared, a total of three leaves on a total of ten dogwood trees. I did everything I could to save those trees, but all of them died. Ten dead dogwoods, one dead hard maple, five live silver maples.

The credit for the trees that lived belongs to Crystal. Lover of insects, arborist of the year, Johnny Appleseed of silver maples. Crystalline Crystal with the magic planting touch, casting her shadow on my black thumb.

Expediency as Deadly Sin

Juanita Brooks is generous to Brigham Young:

> Brigham Young cannot be too seriously criticized if he did consent to sacrifice Lee. The fact was clear that Lee was caught, that he had participated in the massacre, that he was the one who had persuaded the emigrants to leave their wagons. This made him the natural one upon whom to place the responsibility. If by executing him the whole affair could be closed, why not make the sacrifice?...
>
> To air this horrible massacre further would do damage to the church itself and its leaders, since no one now [in 1877] could understand the smoldering fires of hate, the deep emotions of that fall of 1857; "the spirit of the times," the members of the Nauvoo Legion called it.

John Doyle Lee died so the church could live. He died an expedient death. Numberless Mormons were guilty, the fifty perps, one of them John Doyle Lee. The many inciters, one of them George A. Smith. The bishops of the church, the officers of the militia, Brigham's minions in Salt Lake City, Brigham Young himself.

Lee died for them all. Sacrificed so they could flourish, so the church could flourish, so Brigham could flourish. Beside all that, the life of one man was a small price to pay. A necessary cost. Another drop of red ink in the ledger. Blood red ink. Just one more drop.

Part X
Operations and Hospitals

The Power of Prophecy

He blamed Brigham. John Doyle Lee knew Brigham had scripted the trial, had arranged for the verdict, had made the execution inevitable, his execution, the execution of John Doyle Lee. Who else could have it been?

This much he knew, and he proved it for all time, using his power of prophecy. John Doyle Lee in concert with the Lord, as recounted by Jon Krakauer, in his book *Under the Banner of Heaven*:

> According to a family memoir, shortly before Lee was executed he prophesied, "If I am guilty of the crime for which I am convicted, I will go down and out and never be heard of again. If I am not guilty, Brigham Young will die within one year! Yes, within six months."
>
> On August 23, 1877, exactly five months after Lee's death, Brigham was overcome with fever, gastrointestinal cramps, diarrhea, and vomiting. Six days later "The Old Boss," as Lee called him, was dead, most likely from a ruptured appendix.

Nothing happens by accident in the Mormon world. A saint in prophecy is a saint in prayer, a saint in concert with the Lord. When Brigham died, Lee's words became true, true in the eyes of the Mormon God. By causing Brigham to die according to Lee's prophecy, God was saying that John Doyle Lee was not guilty of the Mountain Meadows Massacre.

Will Bagley blames Brigham for the massacre. In his book, one of the latest books on the massacre, *Blood of the Prophets: Brigham Young and the Massacre at Mountain Meadows*, Will Bagley says "Claiming that Brigham Young had nothing to do with Mountain Meadows is akin to arguing that Abraham Lincoln had nothing to do with the Civil War." However imprecise the logic behind it, the statement is basically true.

Abraham Lincoln did not instigate the Civil War. Nor did he condone the massacre of innocent men, women, and children. Abraham Lincoln emancipated the slaves and defended the Constitution of the United States of America, the Constitution that grants to all Americans the right to "life, liberty, and the pursuit of happiness." The right to freedom of speech. The separation of church and state. Brigham Young had no such aims in mind.

But Will Bagley is correct about Brigham Young's guilt. Despite his flawed analogy, his fuzzy thinking, his careless writing, and his deafness to nuance, he got this one thing right. Brigham Young had everything to do with the Mountain Meadows Massacre.

Six Feet Under

2004, May, the second, a Sunday, 8:45 p.m. Sheila and I are locked in our bedroom, watching TV, watching *Six Feet Under*. I am mostly bored, but Sheila is passionately involved.

Someone knocks on the door. A pale voice, a crying voice, implores, "Mom. Mom."

Mom was not to be interrupted. "Go away. We are watching our show." Technically, it is not our show. Technically our show is *The Sopranos*, the show we are both passionate about, the show with enough tension, misbehavior, and retribution to interest me. Enough discipline and payback to engage *I*'s attention, to engage his imagination and fertilize his fantasy life. In my eyes, in the eyes of *I*, *Six Feet Under* is thin barley water compared to *The Sopranos*.

Sheila tells her-of-the-pale-voice to go away. We will talk to her later. We are watching our show, and when our show is over, we will be watching our other show.

"My stomach hurts, Momma." The voice belongs to Chuckie, to Rebekkah, eleven years old, the child, the baby in the family, my little girl.

"Go away," says Sheila. "We are watching our show."

Rebekkah goes back downstairs still crying. A minute passes, two minutes, then Melanie knocks on the door. "Rebekkah has a stomachache," she says. "She is lying on the living room floor crying."

"I said we are watching our show. Go away," says Sheila.

"I'll go," I say and head downstairs. Chuckie is on the floor, crying, holding her belly, curled in a fetal position.

Crystal is laughing. The family comedian, she thinks Chuckie's performance is comic, hilarious, a guy stepping on a banana. I am not amused, nor is I, who barks, "Shut up, Crystal! This isn't funny."

I ask Rebekkah where it hurts. It hurts everywhere. I roll her onto her back, against her wishes. All of this is against Chuckie's wishes. Her stomach hurts, is making her cry. She wants it to stop, wants someone to help, wants to be left alone. She hates everything and everyone.

I press on her stomach, ask if it hurts. "Yes, it hurts." Her voice is plaintive, whining.

I move my fingers around, press on the left side. "Does this hurt?"

"Yes, it hurts! I told you it hurts!" She is angry, crying angry tears.

I press in the middle, in the area of Chuckie's belly button. "Does this hurt?"

"Yes, it hurts. It all hurts." Frustration and anger and tears.

I move my fingers around some more, press on the right side. Rebekkah cries out in pain, jerks her body away, strikes out at my hand.

This time I do not ask if it hurts. I pick up the phone, talk to the answering service, leave a message for the doctor on duty, wait two minutes, go upstairs two steps at a time, put on my shoes, tell Sheila I called the doctor, that I am not waiting, that we are going to the ER. Chuckie Walker is suffering acute appendicitis.

Faith-Based History

2004, June, the eleventh, 5:25 a.m. I am sitting in my home office, my office at the Pond House, pondering Mormon history. I have been pondering it for almost five years now, since I picked up that copy of The Book of Mormon, in that motel room in Kansas, back at the beginning of the year 2000, the year that changed my life.

I am pondering the guilt of Brigham Young, the guilt that cannot be proved. I have formulated a thesis based on my study of Mormon history.

History exists in books, Mormon history too. In books—and on other pieces of paper—historical documents, the primary sources and the so-called primary sources, the documents one studies if one is doing "original" research.

Some of them are not primary. Only a few documents are actual primary sources, the ones that made the actual history. Documents that were the triggering events, that are themselves among the things that happened.

Most of them are not. Most of the documents are not what actually happened. They are *accounts* of what happened. Diaries, testimonies, letters, first-person accounts created by the people who were there, the people who made the history, the perpetrators, or second-person accounts, from people who talked to the perps.

Later come the historians, the commentators, the opinion makers, the people who study the primary sources, the so-called primary sources, and the secondary sources. These people write the third-person accounts, the whatever-person accounts, and that is where I come in. My account is a whatever-person account.

The only true primary sources are the events themselves. Everything else is based on perception, on faith. Even the first-person accounts are based on perception. On perception first, and then on faith. Faith in perception, by the perceivers. First a belief in what they saw, then a belief in what they said they saw. A conviction that what they said they saw is what they saw. That what they saw is what actually happened. What people think of as history is actually a fabrication based on faith, on a faith based on a perception.

That is my thesis, that history is faith-based. All history, all histories, all "his stories." That is what history is, his story. No matter who *his* is, history is his story, his idea of what happened, of what was going on. You may call it her story if you wish.

First-person accounts are his stories. Based on perceptions of what might have actually been. All later accounts are also his stories, based on the earlier his stories. Perceptions based on perceptions. The actual history is gone, what actually happened, and no one *knows* what actually happened. They only know what they saw, what they think they saw, what other people saw, what they believe.

What actually happened is only what actually happened. Truth exists only in the physical world, the world of existential reality. Truth is the empirical event. Once an empirical event becomes empirical evidence, it may no longer be true. It has already become a his story. Gossip, rumor, opinion, history, belief are all the same, all one thing.

Deal with it. Your version may express the truth. Your version may not express the truth. You may have to choose among versions. Be skeptical. Look at all the versions and choose the one you believe. If you cannot be sure of the truth, be sure of what you believe. Make up your mind, choose sides.

Bleeding to Death

The same thing happened to me in the fourth grade, when I was ten, in 1950. Chuckie is eleven, in the fifth grade. Everything else is pretty much the same.

I was sitting at my desk at school. I must have been crying because the teacher walked over and asked me, "What's wrong?" Miss St. Clair. The teacher's name was Miss St. Clair, and she walked over and asked me, "What's wrong?"

"Jim hit me in the stomach," I said.

Jim Albert, sitting two desks back, heard what I said. "What?" He had not hit anybody! Not then, not during class. Maybe out on the playground, at recess, once in a while, in self-defense, or if he felt like it. But not here. Not now. The very idea of him hitting anybody!

In the stomach! From two seats back! Innocence and outrage, an insult never to be forgiven. Peter would pay for this.

Miss St. Clair took me to the nurse, picked me up and carried me to the nurse. I remember the softness of her arms and breasts.

The nurse called my mother, my mother called the doctor, the doctor said, "I will meet you at the hospital." Asbury Hospital, in Minneapolis, Minnesota.

The orderly shaved my belly, showed me a bed pan, said, "Can you go?"

"No, I cannot go," I said.

"Can you try?"

I tried, went. The orderly was relieved.

"I am glad I did not have to use this," the orderly said to my mother. Tubes hanging down from a bag, a catheter.

A gauze pad came down on my face, covered my nose and mouth. A nurse told me to count backward from one hundred. I got almost to ninety-six, then was floating above a huge checkerboard that filled a black vastness of space and waved like a blanket or a beach towel undulating in the wind. Then the checkerboard blanket was on top of me, and I was grabbing handfuls, handfuls that overwhelmed my hands, pulling the blanket toward myself and pushing it away, trying to escape, trying to breathe.

Then I felt a hand on my forehead and saw my mother sitting at the side of the bed. "Honey, are you awake? How do you feel?"

I took my bearings, moved my hands around under the blanket, the ordinary hospital blanket. "Why is it so wet? Why is the bed wet?"

My mother pulled the covers aside. Blood was everywhere. I was in the process of bleeding to death.

This time there was no ether, just a needle poked briefly in my stomach to numb the pain. A nurse stood by my head while the doctor opened me back up, found the unsealed blood vessel, sewed it up, sewed my belly back up.

"Why don't they take it out?" I asked the nurse.

"Huh? Take what out?" answered the nurse.

"The needle. The needle that's stuck in my belly."

"Oh, they took it out. They took it out a long time ago," the nurse said.

Gossip as Gospel

The guilt of Brigham Young cannot be proved. The documents relating to the church's role in the massacre are not available. Many of those records were destroyed, anything Brigham and the minions of Brigham could get their hands on. Some records may have survived, some of the primary and secondary sources.

They would be in the archives, the Historical Archives of the Church of Jesus Christ of Latter-day Saints. Today's church throws nothing away. The Mormon Church is obsessed with historical record, and with who sees the record. Some things may never be seen, not by the likes of you and me. Not by Juanita Brooks and Will Bagley. So we have to guess, we have to build our own record based on faith.

That is where the thesis comes in, the thesis that history is based on faith, that Mormon history especially is based on faith. Will Bagley's history of the Mountain Meadows Massacre is built on faith. Faith in the gossip passed down through the ages, faith that Brigham is guilty, faith that John Doyle Lee is guilty.

Gossip has always blamed Brigham, apostate gossip, anti-LDS gossip, gossip directed against the church. Independent-minded gossip, that rare thing that sometimes even comes from inside the church. Bagley's central thesis is based on this gossip, this faith-based gossip. I share this belief. I and *I* know in our heart that Brigham Young is guilty.

But other gossip has always blamed John Doyle Lee. LDS-inspired gossip, gossip based on the version of the massacre scripted by Brigham Young, the official church version, the version that executed John Doyle Lee. Will Bagley believes this gossip too. Bagley says that John Doyle Lee instigated the first attacks, that Lee's plan was to have the Indians alone do all the killing, that Lee led the Indians in their raids against the Fancher Party during the first days of the massacre.

In his *Confessions* Lee says he tried to restrain the Indians. His evidence is convincing, that the Indians called him *yaw guts*, weak heart, cry baby. Would he have told this story if it were untrue? He would not have told this story unless it were true. That is one piece of my faith in John Doyle Lee, that Lee did not make up the story about his nickname.

Will Bagley does not believe John Doyle Lee. He believes the gossip about John Doyle Lee. Lee was among the perps, that much is true. And then everyone else ran away. The darkest perps, the frenzied killers, the planners with the foaming mouths, all of them fled after the massacre—to the mountains, to the desert, to California, to Nevada, to Arizona. Lee stayed behind, worked his farms, cared for his families, succeeded, made something of his life through hard work and devotion. If he were among those darkest with guilt, would he not have run? He would have run.

Envy follows the powerful man, envy and spite, envy and spite and dislike unto hatred, hatred rotting into the desire to destroy, to take away, to undo. Lee was the only man still around, the only one who could be talked about.

And now comes Will Bagley, still talking, still gossiping, still sharing the gossip about John Doyle Lee.

Bagley believes the children, the babies, the Fancher babies spared by the Mormon killers. The ones too young to know what was happening, too young to remember. The ones cared for by the old ladies, the gossipy old ladies of the Mormon world. Here is what one of those ladies says she was told by one of those babies. Will Bagley:

> One of the most compelling [stories] was attributed to the boy identified as "John Calvin Sorrow," actually John Calvin Miller, the eldest son of Joseph and Matilda Miller, who had "picked arrows from his mother's body." The boy saw his grandfather, grandmother, aunt, father, and mother

murdered. "Clenching his little fists," one of the orphan's nurses recalled, "he would burst into a little passionate speech like this: 'When I get to be a man I'll go to the President of the United States and ask for a regiment of soldiers to go and find John D. Lee. But I don't want to have anybody kill him; I want to shoot him myself, for he killed my father. He shot my father in the back, but I would shoot him in the face."

A child prodigy, a frontier genius, a Daniel Webster in diapers? Or a baby rocked in the arms of a gossipy old lady, a woman who hated John Doyle Lee, a woman identified by Will Bagley as "a most estimable lady." The word has two primary meanings, the word *estimable*: (1) one who can be evaluated, (2) one worthy of esteem. Will Bagley is in partial control of the language, using the word in its second sense without considering the first. Gossipy old women are estimable indeed. Worthy of esteem in the conventional, unquestioning mind. Ripe for evaluation by skeptical minds.

The Operation

2004, the second of May, 9:30 p.m. Chuckie, Sheila, and I are at the ER, Melanie and are Crystal at home. The ER doctor is asking questions, listening to answers, probing with his fingers and stethoscope. He orders blood tests, x-rays, an MRI, prescribes pain killers. Time slithers by, ten o'clock, eleven o'clock, midnight. We take turns calling the Pond House to talk to the girls, to reassure them, to make sure they are safe.

"Will Chuckie be OK?" they want to know. "Is she going to have an operation?"

The answer arrives, the diagnosis from the doctor—acute appendicitis, an emergency operation. "The surgeon is on his way. The anesthesiologist is here, the orderly and the nurses are preparing the room."

Everyone ready at three, three a.m., the morning of the third of May. The orderly shaves Chuckie's belly, Chuckie asks questions and watches every move. A shower cap covers her hair.

The anesthesiologist is a friend of mine. The surgeon is the guy who fixed my hernia. He tells us that this is a routine procedure, they do them all the time. It will take forty-five minutes, maybe an hour. "We should be done by three forty-five, four at the latest."

The orderly rolls the gurney toward the operating room, the gurney carrying our little girl, our Chuckie Walker, our little Pearl Prynne. True to that other nickname, she is wise, alert, watchful, ready.

Sheila and I walk down the hall to the waiting room, really just a balcony hanging over the foyer of the hospital, an impromptu waiting room with a couple of chairs, a table, some magazines, *Yankee*, *Smithsonian*, several issues of one of those nostalgic magazines, uplifting celebrations of the past, the way things were, grandmothers cooking Sunday dinner, a ride in the Studebaker. I try to think of simpler times, picking the magazines up and putting them down.

"Litary Atainment"

John Doyle Lee is innocent of the gossip, innocent of most of what they thought he did. He did plenty, is not what I could call an innocent man. He was willing to commit murder, willing to kill innocent people, people who had already been injured. His gun misfired.

But he did not make the plan. He did not script the massacre. He was there, he participated, and when it was over, he stayed around. He did not run. He did not hide from his guilt. He spoke his mind, confessed his sins, absorbed the blame, died so others could live. So Brigham could live. Brigham and his minions, Brigham and the church of which he was the head.

Will Bagley underrates John Doyle Lee, on nearly every page of his book.

I will give you one little example. Bagley mentions a visit to Lonely Dell by a Mormon missionary, William Solomon. Lonely Dell, where Lee lived in Arizona late in his life, just before his capture. Lonely Dell, at Lee's Ferry, the crossing of the Colorado River at the head of the Grand Canyon, the place where many rafting trips of today put into the river. According to Will Bagley, "Solomon overestimated [Lee's] 'great litary Atainment,' but he found Lee 'full of energy and determination in the building up of the Kingdom of God upon the earth.'" Still. After many betrayals, by Brigham and his minions, by the leaders of his church, John Doyle Lee was still working to build the Kingdom of Moroni upon the earth.

Lee had almost no formal education. He taught himself to read, taught others to read, kept meticulous accounts, kept diaries all his life, wrote his *Confessions*, his autobiography. Here is one paragraph from that book, from *The Confessions of John Doyle Lee*, one typically well-written paragraph, John Doyle Lee's description of Joseph Smith:

> Joseph Smith was a most extraordinary man; he was rather large in stature, some six feet two inches in height, well built, though a little stoop shouldered, prominent and well developed features, a Roman nose, light chestnut hair, upper lip full and rather protruding, chin broad and square, an eagle eye, and on the whole there was something in his manner and appearance that was bewitching and winning; his countenance was that of a plain, honest man, full of benevolence and philanthropy and devoid of deceit or hypocrisy. He was resolute and firm of purpose, strong as most men in physical power, and all who saw him were forced to admire him, as he then looked and existed.... In every gathering he was a welcome guest, and always added to the amusement of the people, instead of dampening their ardor.

Lee wrote neither novels nor poems, published nothing, neither large nor small, during his lifetime. Wrote his *Confessions* on death row, awaiting his execution. Revised nothing. His sentences, compound and complex, are graceful and balanced, rife with parallelism. William Solomon was right. A whole lot righter than Will Bagley. All things considered, it looks like "great litary Atainment" to me.

Infection Everywhere

Three forty-five. The anesthesiologist came out and kneeled by the chairs in the waiting room, the waiting balcony. He said, "The appendix is out, that part is over. It was the size and color of a plum—a very ripe plum. But we found a lot of infection, spreading everywhere."

The operation was not over. They had to go in again, make another incision, deal with the infected tissue.

Four thirty went by, five o'clock. Finally the surgeon came out to give his report to the parents, but first he had some questions. "I think you said the pain hit her suddenly, in the evening. Are you sure of that? Was she fine during the day? No complaints, no dragging around, no loss of energy?"

We looked at each other, trying to recall that day now so long ago. We remembered how she ran around the yard, played with her sisters, did cartwheels. We remembered no problems on Saturday either, or on Friday, the day before the day before. Everything had seemed normal, Chuckie's energy running high, her spirits off the chart, then the sudden blitzkrieg pain last night.

The surgeon was surprised. "With all that infection, there should have been some clear indication—discomfort, a stomachache, lassitude, vomiting, something." Or maybe she is just a strong girl, stoic, forebearing.

He said he had had to take out some small bowel, some large bowel, from the area surrounding the appendix. There would be a biopsy. He was sorry, but it could be lymphoma, maybe Crohn's Disease.

Lymphoma. A painless cancerous disease of unknown cause. An unspoken promise of a short life, a lingering death. "We will not know until Wednesday. You can sleep in the room. We will bring in an extra bed."

"One of These Days I'm Going to Cut You into Little Pieces"

We took turns sleeping in the room. I woke there on Wednesday morning still waiting for the results of the biopsy. Sheila arrived at 8:30 to relieve me.

"How is she?" Rebekkah was still sleeping, still deep in her drug coma.

"The same. Everything is the same. Her temperature spiked briefly, then it went back down. Everything is about the same. How are you?"

"I could use a cup of coffee." Sheila would be taking over. I would get her coffee then go home, shower, dress for work.

I went into the hall. The coffee shop was not open yet, but the nurses had been solicitous, generous with coffee or soda. I walked down to the nursing station, waited for the nurse and the lady in charge of records to finish talking. It dawned on me that they were gossiping. They had a lot to say about someone, about several someones. People they knew, maybe even coworkers, had done things that needed discussion, sorting out, evaluation, possibly condemnation.

Eventually the nurse looked my way, a silent look, unwelcoming.

I tried to smile. "Could I get a cup of coffee for my wife?"

The nurse looked at me for a still moment, one of those looks, then asked, "Who is your wife?"

"Sheila. My wife is Sheila. I thought you knew." Silence.

The lady at the desk tried to help. "You're with Rebekkah," she said.

"How is she doing this morning?" More silence from the nurse, that *do-not-meddle-with-me* look.

I started to back away, putting on an act of mock self-abnegation. "No, no," I said, "I'm sorry, what was I thinking, I can see that I am interrupting, you are busy, I should not have bothered you, let's just skip the whole thing," backing away, seething, into Chuckie's room.

I sat in the chair and simmered. Sheila could tell that something had gone wrong. "What happened?" she asked. I glared at her, my thoughts on the nurse: maybe her throat, just rip it out, or a garbage disposal—no, a wood chipper, just stuff her in.

Then the nurse herself marched in, a cup of coffee in her hand, already preaching. "You have to understand, sir, that people who don't belong here try to get free coffee from us, and we must be careful." Visiting hours three hours away. I was still grindy from spending the night, my hair sticking up in odd directions. What strangers could be here? Did she think I had arrived by spaceship, by transponder, did I drop down from the moon?

But no, I was not there. I was not around any more. *I* was there. *I* said to the nurse, "Shut the fuck up! Get the fuck out of here!" *I* in full battle mode, Tony Soprano, Sammy the Bull Gravano, Paulie Walnuts, Christopher Moltisanto, Samuel L. Jackson in *Pulp Fiction*, ready to kill the nurse, eager to burn her with coffee and tear out her guts.

Sheila said, "Oh, Jesus." She had seen this before. Sheila had been acquainted with *I*.

"Sir, if you continue to use that language, I will call my supervisor."

"I will throw your supervisor through the window," *I* said. "And you too, but not before I break both your arms."

Then I grabbed my jacket, headed down the hallway toward home.

Later that day, I was back in the room when the surgeon showed up. The supervisor of nurses was with him. They wondered if I was all right, if there had been a problem.

The three of us went to the lounge to talk it over, the surgeon and the supervisor of nurses and me. I said I was sorry; I had over-reacted. Maybe it was the fear and the worrying that had caught up with me. I talked about Rebekkah. I put my face in my hands to cover my tears.

The supervisor of nurses touched my hand. "Don't be hard on yourself. We see this now and then. You are under a lot of stress. I will speak to the nurse. She should have been more sensitive."

Part XI
History and Theology

The Oppressive Weight of Mormon History

I want to say it. I want to say, "that was then and this is now." I want to say that today's Church of Jesus Christ of Latter-day Saints is a different church, a church based on love, on inclusion, on turning the other cheek, on monogamy. If not always on lifetime monogamy, at least on one marriage at a time.

I lived myself in the Kingdom of Moroni for six months, in the year 2000, on my way from one monogamous marriage to another. I liked Salt Lake City. In many ways it is a nice place to live. I loved the landscape, the desert and the mountains, the intersection of water and sand. The clear air of the city, that western light, the nearness of Nevada.

I will not be living there again. I did not love the orderliness carried to an extreme, the white shirts and frocks and cars. The righteousness, the exclusiveness; the missionary spirit, the bishops, the elders, the shining temples and stakes. The oppressive weight of Mormon belief, the oppressive weight of Mormon history, the inescapable conjunction of Mormon faith and history.

All history is based on faith, the faith of the teller in his own perceptions, the perceptions of the historian. Some Mormon history is doubly based on faith. Faith-based by being written by a human perceiver and faith-based by being written by a Mormon believer.

For example, the official centennial history of the Mormon state of Utah, written by Thomas G. Alexander and published in 1996. Thomas

G. Alexander does the faith-based dance, the double-jointed, faith-based dance of the official Mormon historian. Here is one of his steps:

> The erroneous impression has persisted, especially in areas distant from Utah, that members of the Church of Jesus Christ of Latter-day Saints practice polygamy and religiously sanctioned murder.... Often the media and casual readers give little attention to the distinction between the fundamentalist groups they call "Mormons" and the Latter-day Saints, whose orthodox members have tried to disown these practices for nearly a century. Nevertheless, thousands of Latter-day Saints have been confronted unjustly by antagonists at home and abroad who are repelled by the immorality and violence of such customs and who insist that the LDS Church and its associates practice polygamy and even engage in ritual murder.

I notice two phrases, phrases that look like the key to what I think is the truth about polygamy and blood atonement. One phrase is this: "for nearly a century." The other phrase is this: "have tried to disown."

"Orthodox members have tried to disown these practices for nearly a century." Since about the time of statehood. Utah became a state in 1896. Thomas G. Alexander published his book in 1996. Thus: "orthodox members have tried to disown these practices for nearly a century."

Polygamy. The church has tried three times to disown the practice of polygamy. Polygamy was *publicly disavowed* by the church in 1890, in "the Manifesto of the Apostles," better known as "The First Manifesto." Many church leaders refused to sign, so enamored were they of their many-wived lives.

Polygamy became *illegal* in 1895. In Utah, in the soon-to-be-state of Utah, in the constitution for the future state of Utah. Life went on in the individual, multitudinous Mormon home.

Polygamy was *forbidden* in 1904. Finally. By the church. Officially, publicly, and privately. In "The Second Manifesto." Since then all polygamists have been breakers of both laws, the law of the state and the law of the church. Today polygamy is practiced by only a few fundamentalist hicks. A few hundred fundamentalist hicks in the mountains of southwestern Utah and northwestern Arizona. On the barren desert lands of southwestern Texas. A few hundred frequently murderous fundamentalist hicks hiding in the desert and the mountains. Murderous, polygamous hicks who could not exist but for the oppressive weight of Mormon history.

Polygamy was formally disowned, doubly or triply formally disowned. Blood atonement was never formally disowned. Blood atonement never existed. According to the church. According to the Church of Jesus Christ of Latter-day Saints, there never was a doctrine of blood atonement. Thus: it could not be disowned.

This is logic, hard work in the field of logic. Hard work in the field of being, in the field of being and not-being. Metaphysical work, hard metaphysical work.

The logic is clear. Something that does not exist cannot be disowned, no matter how hard one tries. The difference between trying to disown and disowning is the difference between failure and success. Logic says that the church failed to disown blood atonement because blood atonement never existed.

Blood atonement existed. That is why Thomas G. Alexander says the church has tried to disown it. It existed in reality. It existed in the words of Joseph Smith and in the words of Brigham Young. I have told you about all of this. Blood atonement existed, and the church has tried mightily and long to disown it. Tried and failed.

And polygamy? What does it mean to say that "for nearly a century," "orthodox members have *tried to disown*" polygamy? It means that they have failed. Tried and failed.

The harder the Mormons try to disown their past, the more it comes back to haunt them.

Waiting for the Word

2004, May, the third, the fourth, the fifth. Monday, Tuesday,

Wednesday. The longest days in the life of the family. Rebekkah was in her hospital bed, silent, indrawn, fighting against the pain. Pushing on her button, her morphine button. She was allowed to take a hit of morphine whenever she wanted—once a day or twenty times an hour, even two times each minute. The machine made sure she did not overdose.

She had had major surgery—double major surgery, two incisions, one for the appendix and one for the infection. Now some of the tissue they removed was over in York, at the lab, being biopsied. The technicians were checking for lymphoma, for Crohn's Disease.

Sheila slept in Chuckie's room some nights, and I slept at home. I slept in Chuckie's room the other nights, and Sheila slept at home. Melanie and Crystal slept at home every night, got up and went to school in the morning and came back home in the afternoon.

When I had to be in the office or teaching class, Sheila stayed in Chuckie's room. When Sheila was teaching, I stayed in Chuckie's room. The doctor came and went, the nurses were in and out—drawing blood and checking the IVs, all three of the IVs. One for nutrition, one for infection, one for pain.

Rebekkah was holding her own, Chuckie Walker, holding it all inside, holding her insides together. Watching the nurses, watching the needles, observing the holes in her arms. Keeping count of the needle-sticks. To the nurses and the doctor, she was a wonderful patient. She put up with everything, never complained, never yelped in pain.

To her parents she was a terrible patient. Impatient with touch, with talk, with consolation. Almost the first words out of her mouth when she started to talk years ago were these: "Yeve me a-yone." "Don't yook at me." "Get away." Now these seemed the only words from her mouth.

Sheila would arrive in the morning. "How are you feeling, honey?"

"Don't look at me." That or a silent stare, a baleful stare.

I would smooth Chuckie's hair, try to plant a kiss. "Leave me alone. Get away." Or that baleful stare.

The long-faced parents slumping down in the bedside chair.

"Still no news," the doctor kept saying. "We may know something on Wednesday."

The Enduring Legacy

Mormon fundamentalism is the old Mormonism, the way it used to be. The modern church has disowned polygamy, blood atonement, racism, all sorts of medieval practices. That does not mean those practices have ceased to exist. It does not mean they never existed. It does not mean they will not exist again.

Jon Krakauer is the author of the best new book on Mormonism, *Under the Banner of Heaven*, the book depicting the legacy of the fathers: their treatment of women, their administration of justice, their conversations with God. Joseph and Brigham, the fathers of Mormonism, the enduring legacy of the fathers of Mormonism.

1984, July, the twenty-fourth. American Fork, Utah. The Lafferty boys, pious Mormon fundamentalists, sons of their father, brought up according to the way. Here is what two of the Lafferty boys did on that day, Ron the theorist, Dan the butcher. Jon Krakauer interviewed the butcher:

> [Dan] still insists he is innocent of any crime, but, paradoxically, does not deny that he killed Brenda and Erica. When asked to explain how both these apparently contradictory statements can be true, he says, "I was doing God's will, which is not a crime."
>
> Lafferty isn't reticent about describing exactly what happened on July 24, 1984. He says that shortly after noon, he, Ron, and the two drifters who had been traveling with them, Ricky Knapp and Chip Carnes, drove to the apartment of his youngest brother, Allen, in American Fork, twenty minutes down the interstate from where he is now imprisoned. Inside the brick duplex he found his fifteen-month-old niece, Erica, standing in her crib, smiling up at him. "I spoke to her for a minute," Lafferty recalls. "I told her 'I'm not sure what this

is all about, but apparently it's God's will that you leave this world; perhaps we can talk about it later.'" And then he ended her life with a ten-inch boning knife.

After dispatching Erica, he calmly walked into the kitchen and used the same knife to kill the baby's mother. Now, seventeen years after committing these two murders, he insists, very convincingly, that he has never felt any regret for the deed, or shame.

Like his older brother, Ron, Dan Lafferty was brought up as a pious Mormon. "I've always been interested in God and the Kingdom of God," he says. "It's been the center of my focus since I was a young child." And he is certain God intended for him to kill Brenda and Erica Lafferty: "It was like someone had taken me by the hand that day and led me comfortably through everything that happened. Ron had received a revelation from God that these lives were to be taken. I was the one who was supposed to do it. And if God wants something to be done, it will be done. You don't want to offend Him by refusing to do His work."

An uppity woman. The Will of God. Blood atonement. The legacy of that old-time religion alive and well in Utah in 1984.

Chuckie's Theology

Chuckie explained her theology to me on a winter's morn, early in 2004. I was in my home office. Rebekkah, just out of bed and still in her PJs, came to find me, to say hello and get a hug. We got to talking. For some unremembered reason, the odd notion of an after-life came up, and Chuckie Walker explained her theology to me:

> When you die you go to heaven and become an angel. If you are a good angel, you get to go back to earth and live some more.
>
> If you are a bad angel, you go to hell.
>
> If you were a good angel and you go back to earth and

*A Child Said, What Is the Grass?,
Fetching It to Me on Her Head*

you shoot someone or do something bad, you go to the devil. If he accepts you, you go to hell. If he rejects you, you go back to earth. If they reject you, it is all over.

If earth accepts you and someone shoots you in the leg or something bad happens, you go back to heaven and they give you a test to see if you are good enough.

If you are not good enough, you go to hell.

If you are good enough, you go to the other heaven. You get to live in a cloud house. You get a flying wheelchair because of your leg.

Reverence for the Priesthood

Brenda Lafferty was an uppity woman, an educated woman, independent. Jon Krakauer quotes Brenda's older sister Betty: "'Brenda was the only one of the Lafferty wives who was educated,' Betty points out. 'And her education was what they were afraid of. Because Brenda was confident in her beliefs, and her sense of right and wrong, and she wasn't about to let anyone take that away from her. She felt it was her duty to defend the other women. She was their only hope.'"

Brenda knew her mind. She lived in the real world. She stood up to Ron Lafferty, argued with him, tried to awaken his brothers, including her husband, Allen. Her behavior was in violation of the preaching of Brigham Young, in violation of the rules governing the behavior of women as set down by Brigham Young in a sermon delivered to the faithful on the seventh of June, 1846, in Iowa, at the start of the great migration westward. John Doyle Lee summarized the sermon in his diary:

> It is the duty of all my wives & all other women to mind their own business—keep themselves—houses or tents clean & not to dictate my business of the Priesthood or want to know where I am going or where I slept last night.... It is their duty to bear all the children they can lawfully & raise them up in the name of the Lord watching over them & seeing

that they are kept from playing with ungodly children from falling in rivers or exposing themselves to sickness & dangers & teaching them to reverence the Priesthood & when she has raised up to deliver them up to their fathers....

To which Juanita Brooks adds: "A man was to hold himself above the whims of any woman, and while he should treat his wives with kindness and tenderness, he should not allow them to sway his decisions or deflect him from his duty. Brother Brigham always spoke with consummate scorn of any man who should bend to the will of a wife."

But no scorn for the woman who would bend to the will of her husband. Or to the will of any member of the priesthood. For example, Elizabeth Smart. A fourteen-year-old Mormon girl abducted from her home in Salt Lake City, in the middle of the night, on the fifth of June, 2002, and held captive for nine months by Brian David Mitchell, a Mormon fundamentalist convinced that God had ordered him to take seven virgin brides. Elizabeth was the first.

Elizabeth knew her kidnapper as the handyman who had worked for her father. While doing some chores around the family house, Brian David Mitchell had seen Elizabeth, had looked her over, had liked what he saw. Brian David Mitchell and his God liked what they saw, and so they talked it over. God told Brian David to get Elizabeth from her home, take her as the first of seven virgin brides.

Brian David crept into the house in the middle of the night and abducted Elizabeth from her bedroom at knifepoint. He took her into the woods behind the house, married her in a ceremony conducted by his regular wife, Barzee, consummated the marriage then and there and against Elizabeth's will, then set about converting her to his ways.

Police found Elizabeth the following March. She was walking down a street in Salt Lake City with Brian David and Barzee Mitchell. She would not admit to being Elizabeth. She did not want to return home. Jon Krakauer explains how Brian David accomplished her conversion:

Using his gift for fundamentalist doctrine and adroitly manipulating the religious indoctrination Elizabeth had received since she was old enough to talk, Mitchell cowed the girl into becoming an utterly submissive polygamous concubine—buttressing his powers of theological persuasion with threats to kill her and her family. Raised to obey Mormon authority unquestioningly, and to believe that LDS doctrine is the law of God, she would have been particularly susceptible to the dexterous fundamentalist spin Mitchell applied to familiar Mormon scripture.

Wallace Stegner has commented on the "essentially fundamentalist hostility to free thought" inherent in Mormon life. Freedom of thought: bad enough when found in a boy, never to be tolerated from a girl.

The First Report

The report came back late Wednesday afternoon, the first biopsy report, from the lab in York. The news was good and bad, definitely good and tentatively bad. Chuckie Walker was not dying from lymphoma, but she would be a life-long sufferer of Crohn's Disease. "Probably." Probably she would have permanently distressed intestines, upper and lower. Her digestion would never be right. She would never eat normally. She was likely to die before her time. Probably all this would be so.

"What do you mean, *probably?*" Sheila asked. "What kind of biopsy report is this?"

"The pathologists are not completely sure, but to them it looks like Crohn's Disease," the doctor replied.

"So what do you think?" I asked. "Is it Crohn's?"

"Well, they are not completely sure," said the doctor. "But yes, that would be my diagnosis."

Sheila was sure. "We need a second opinion," she said.

The doctor looked at Sheila. "Well, we can send the tissue to Washington," he said. "To the NIH. They are the best, so they wil know for sure."

"Send it to Washington," Sheila said.

Chuckie and Basketball

Saturday, the twenty-first of February, 2004. Chuckie and I were lying on the bed watching the Carolina game, the second game with Florida State University. Carolina was ahead by seventeen in the first half. Chuckie had a question. "Who is the best team in basketball?"

Chuckie had just turned eleven. She didn't know much yet about basketball, but I was teaching her. She could already say, "Duke sucks."

"I don't know," I answered. "Duke is irritatingly good again."

"Duke is the best team in basketball this year?"

"I hope not. It might be Stanford. But Duke has the most good players, and they are well coached. By a squirrel, but still. So among college teams, yeah, they might be the best. Except for Stanford."

"What about the pro teams?"

"Hmmm?" I had switched channels, first to the Syracuse-Georgetown game, then to Baylor-Missouri. "What did you ask? The best pro team? Maybe Sacramento, the Kings. I love to watch Minnesota, and the Lakers are a cliché, like Duke. But I guess Sacramento is the best right now."

"Look!" Chuckie was surprised. "No one is at that game. Who is playing now?"

"That's Baylor and Missouri."

"Where are they playing?"

"At Baylor," I said. The camera had backed away from a close-up, and we could see a lot of empty green seats. "Wow," I said, "you're right. No one's there."

"Would you go if you lived there?"

"Yeah, I'd go. What else would I do in Waco, Texas? But I wouldn't want to work at Baylor."

"Why not?"

"It's not a very good school. It's a Baptist place."

"What's that?"

"The school is run by the Southern Baptist Church."

By then we were back to the Carolina game. The lead had shrunk to six. I was bleeding Carolina blue.

"So is Sacramentolio, whatever, number one?"

"Huh? Oh, the best pro team. Well, there really isn't a number one in the NBA, but right now I think Stanford is number one in college."

"Would you like to see Stanford play?"

"Yeah, I would love it."

"Well, I have four passes, and I will sell them to you. I mean six, I have six passes."

"Great. I would love to go. Who are they playing?"

"The Kings, the Saccoro-whatevers. It's the best game. I have six passes, so you can take your homeys. You can go backstage too."

"Wow, backstage. My homeys would love that."

"But you have to give me your dog."

"You're charging me my dog for the tickets to the Stanford-Sacramento game?"

"Yes. You have to give me your dog."

"No. The deal is off. No way you get the dog."

The Hand of God in Human Affairs

God told Ron Lafferty that Brenda must die, and Erica, Brenda's fifteen-month-old daughter. Brenda was hindering the progress of Mormon fundamentalism, so Brenda and Erica had to die. God told Ron that it was so. Ron, the family theorist, told Dan, the family butcher. So Dan killed Erica and Brenda. With his boning knife, in the name of the fundamentalist Mormon God, on orders from God.

God has always been active in Mormon affairs. God spoke directly to Joseph Smith, the original Mormon prophet. God revealed his will to Joseph, and Joseph revealed God's will to the faithful. God also spoke through actions and signs. In the time of Joseph and in the time of Brigham Young.

Juanita Brooks tells a story about Brigham, about Brigham and his first wife Agatha, about the hand of God.

> Agatha became upset over family affairs. Either she had not known that her husband had taken his [most recent] wives, Polly and Lavina Young, or she was ill with the thought that he was courting or paying too much attention to another. She railed out at him and scolded and abused the whole group, until he in turn rebuked her and predicted that she would yet feel the chastening hand of the lord. Within a few minutes she became violently ill and continued to suffer great pains until he laid his hands on her head and blessed her, at which she was relieved and fell asleep.

If only Brenda Lafferty had repented in a swoon. If only God had come down when Dan raised his boning knife to Brenda. If only God had made Brenda violently ill and someone, maybe the fundamentalist prophet Brian David Mitchell, had laid hands upon her head. If only.

The Second Report

Washington said no. The pathologists at the NIH said Chuckie would be fine. No signs of lymphoma, no signs of Crohn's Disease. Chuckie's appendix had been seriously inflamed, seriously infected, but only in the normal way. Just a bad case of appendicitis.

Since then she has grown about a foot. Chuckie Walker. Over the summer Chuckie Walker sprouted up like a barnyard weed, skinny as a broomstick.

She is now as tall as her older sisters. She is still slightly pigeon-toed, which makes her walk like a filly. She still does cartwheels. She still runs like the wind. She still is as beautiful as a dream.

She will start sixth grade this coming Wednesday. Wednesday the first of September. In the year 2004. Is it a sign from God?

Part XII
Mormon Women, Family Cats

An Interlude of Introspection and Philosophy

2004, Monday, the twenty-fifth of October. John Berryman's birthday. 1914. The American poet John Berryman was born on the twenty-fifth of October in 1914. He died on the seventh of January, 1972. Fifty-seven years old. Suicide.

Winter in Minneapolis. A cold morning. John Berryman walked out on the Washington Avenue Bridge, waved to a person who happened to be there, then jumped. Not into the river, which may or may not have been covered with ice, but onto the ground. The frozen ground, probably covered here and there with snow. He landed near or on the railroad tracks. The body was identified by his name having been embossed on his eyeglasses case.

I am not sure why I am writing this. I guess my imagination was tweaked by today's date, which happens to be the ninetieth anniversary of John Berryman's birth. And death is pretty much always on my mind. The death of John Berryman and all the other dead people I ever knew. I call him John because that is what I called him when he was alive. I and *I*, except that he never met *I*. The character I call *I*. *I* was around, *I* has been around almost as long as I have, but John Berryman never met *I*. He knew me instead.

"Who cares?" you may be asking. Me, I am answering. Me and *me*. And maybe Delores.

Delores is on my chest as I write these words of deathless prose. Ha ha. Deathless prose is one of my jokes. No prose is deathless, certainly not these days. Anything written in seriousness and art is dead before it is born these days. The joke is based on irony, and the joke is bitter. I want my prose to be deathless. But it is no more deathless than I. I and *I*.

Delores is alive, alive and sleeping on my chest as I slump down in my ergonomic chair and write these words. John Berryman is dead, dead now for thirty-four years, ten months, eighteen days. The coming together of Delores and John Berryman is a coincidence, a mental coincidence, something that happened in my brain when I noticed the date as Delores was crawling up onto my chest.

Out of such coincidences arises the meaning of life, human life. Surely the meaning of life in the case of Delores and all the other cats is matter of coincidence, something like coincidence. Some fundamentalist idiots might disagree with that, but I think no reputable theologians would.

But human life? Surely smart people exist who think human life has meaning beyond a series and pattern of coincidences, but I think those people are wrong. Though I recognize the danger and absolute finitude of an existence based on the concept of coincidence, that is the existence I believe in and prefer.

The coincidence, for example, that brought me to Salt Lake City. The coincidence that had Sheila and Melanie and Crystal and Rebekkah and Delores all living there. The coincidence that had Sheila and me living in emotional situations that made us ready for just the coincidence that brought us together.

The coincidence, for a second example, of Mormonism, that Salt Lake City happened to be the capital of the Kingdom of Moroni. Without those coincidences, I would not be writing these words today. And I like my words, my project. I like putting my family life in the context of Mormonism. This is one of the things that gives meaning to my life today, this series of coincidences.

But now I need to say something about Mormonism. Because the sections alternate, more or less, and the present section is personal, more or less, sort of about the family, I must now go on to say something about Mormonism.

Something to Do with Mormonism

No, wait. I just remembered a thread from earlier, from when I was talking about Chuckie Walker's appendicitis, about her operation. When I was talking about that, I mentioned a coincidence. That Chuckie had her appendix out at almost the exact same age and under almost the exact same conditions as I had my appendix taken out—lo!—about half a century earlier.

Then I went back to Chuckie's adventure, built to some moments of high drama and suspense, and explained how all that was resolved. Then I talked about what happened later, when she was well again. But I did not tell you what happened after I was well again.

The story is simple enough. I was attacked by appendicitis during school. I was sitting at my desk in Miss St. Clair's fourth-grade class. Suddenly the pain was unbearable. The teacher said, "What's wrong?"

I said, "Jim Albert hit me in the stomach."

She said, "Jim has been sitting right there all morning; he couldn't have hit you in the stomach."

I said, "Oh I don't know," and then I cried some more.

The teacher took me to the nurse, and the nurse called my mother, and my mother took me to the hospital, and the doctor took out my appendix, but he left some arteries unsewn, so I almost bled to death, but then I got fixed again and survived and got better.

It seems like many days and weeks went by before I returned to school. I had gotten skinny. I was weak. Jim Albert was waiting. He knocked me down and sat on my stomach and beat the crap out of me. All the girls in the class danced around us and sang a song. The song took the form of a medieval rondeau and said, "Stitt is crying, / Look at his tears."

Over the following summer I grew about a foot in height. Just as Chuckie Walker did after her operation. But I did not put on any weight and I never got back at Jim Albert. Instead I developed a new friend. A new character in my life. The character I call *I*. That mean guy was born at that time. At that time and a lot of other times pretty dern much like it.

Here's the Deal with Delores

Delores is the ur-cat, the founder of the whole dern Walker family cat clan, the mother of the Utah litter. She had a wonderful life back there, lying under the bed with her babies at her breasts. Then someone put her in a truck and drove her cross country. Then her babies started to die in unpleasant ways. Then other cats appeared, farm cats crossing the road from the barn, feral cats wandering up from the woods. A couple of these cats, Misty and Ginger (*zhon-ZHAY*), were deemed worthy and allowed into the house, into Delores's house.

Delores saw her world falling apart. Strangers were everywhere, eating her food, sleeping in her bed, using her litter. Eventually she adapted by keeping her distance, watching suspiciously from afar, hissing a lot.

Then the pregnant one showed up, the one we named "Mom Cat," the skinny, disgusting one sick with feline leukemia. That one showed up and birthed three kittens on the kitchen floor, so Delores went to live in the garage. She slept on an old roll of insulation. She lapped water from a puddle. She pooped and peed in the woods. She ran in terror whenever I came home in the car.

Then the kittens went away. Melanie's friend Robin took one. Barb next door arranged for the other two. I went into therapy mode: I caught Delores and brought her inside. I held her in my arms and walked her around the house. I showed her that the new creatures were suddenly gone. I did this for several days running.

Now she will come in by herself. And that is how she came to be reclining on my chest earlier this morning, as I sat here writing at my desk in my home office.

I am glad that Delores is better. I am glad that she is back. Delores has had a rough life. She has outlived most of her babies, has watched her world fall apart around her. She deserves a little quiet, a little comfort, deserves to have her ticks removed, her ears scratched, her fur stroked. She deserves to sleep on my chest while I am writing.

The Mormon Women

What to say about the Mormon women? A lot, actually, and it is not a simple subject. I will start with Wallace Stegner, himself neither a Mormon nor a woman, but a student of Mormonism. A significant American writer. A writer of deathless prose. Deathless I guess because his prose is still in print, still being read by the not-yet-dead. Maybe not deathless in that other sense. The sense involving the word *great*.

Wallace Stegner wrote about the American West. He wrote novels, short stories, biographies, all of them concerning the American West in one way or another. He wrote…well, he wrote histories or cultural studies or meditations on peoples and their ways…. I am not sure what to call these other books of his. Among them, whatever they are, are his books about Mormons and Mormonism. He won a Pulitzer Prize.

Here is one thing Wallace Stegner said about Mormonism and Mormon women, a favorite passage of mine: "That I do not accept the faith that possessed [the Mormons] does not mean I doubt their frequent devotion and heroism in its service. Especially their women. Their women were incredible."

Indeed. It was a patriarchal society, invented by and for the men. The women got the worst of it, as I have already told you, in many ways and in many words. My words and the words of Joseph Smith, of Brigham Young.

The word *vassals* comes to mind. The words *serving class*. The words *second class citizens,* if not *third.* The word *objects.* The word *concubine.* The word *polygamy.*

Ah, polygamy. Plural marriage, one man, many wives. Brigham Young said, *none of my wives has any business knowing where I slept last night.*

Mormon Husband, Three Bonneted Wives, Five Children

But he always knew where they slept, and with whom. With him or with the children or alone. Polygamy never meant one woman, many husbands.

But I digress. Or I get ahead of myself. Polygamy is the core subject with regard to Mormonism. It is, in the words of Terryl L. Givens, "the most notorious of [Mormon] religious practices." The one that everyone gets around to talking about. Or back to, as I will, a little later, when I talk about the wives, the Mormon wives, about my favorites among the Mormon wives.

The First Generation of Cats

The story of Delores, the story of the Whole Dern Walker Family Cat Clan, starts back in Salt Lake City, where the Whole Dern Walker Family Clan itself started. The early days of the Walker family cat clan were chronicled by Chuckie Walker. Years ago, judging from the handwriting. Maybe for a school assignment, I don't know.

I found Chuckie's chronicle last June, June of 2004, when I was emptying the upstairs junk room so the guys replacing the furnace could get at the broken radiator in that room.

I found two sheets of school-style writing paper with a chronicle written upon them. The handwriting was that of a child, and I saw lots of mistakes in spelling and grammar and punctuation and word usage.

The chronicle had no title and no author, but at the top of the first sheet of paper was a single-word heading: Rebekkah. Chuckie Walker's real name is Rebekkah, so I knew the chronicle had been written by Chuckie Walker. Probably about three years ago, when she was seven or eight years old and in the second grade at Franklin Township Elementary School in Cashtown, Pennsylvania. Here is the chronicle almost verbatim. I fixed some of the errors to make it comprehensible:

> One time ago in Utah our cat got out of the house. And we didn't know if she would come back. But two days after that we went to the places we could go to. But she did not

come back until four months later and she was bleeding from her butt. And she went straight to her bed and had babies.

She had six of them and we named all of them. But my baby cat was Max. My sister Crystal's was Polkadot and my other sister's was Dudley and the day after that Blackie was born. And that was Peter's cat. And my mommy didn't have one because she liked Delores who was the mommy cat.

But one time ago my cat died because it got hit by a dolly. Now my cat is Happy. And my sister Melanie's cat got hit by a car and now her cat is Monkey. But my sister Crystal doesn't have one because her cat got run over too. I wish they never died. But three died.

I wish Melanie's cat never died because her cat was so cute. And now they are all growing up.

Where is T. S. Eliot now, that master of cat chronicles? Where is Jacques Derrida to decode Chuckie's prose? Will the prose of Chuckie Walker live forever, like the prose of Jacques Derrida (ha ha) and the cat jingles of T. S. Eliot? Or will it get hit by a dolly and run over by a car like the prose of her stepfather?

A Couple of Mormon Women

Wallace Stegner mentions several remarkable Mormon women in his book, *The Gathering of Zion: The Story of the Mormon Trail*. I am going to tell you, really quote you, about two of those women in a minute. First I want to say a few words about the Mormon Trail and the gathering of Zion.

The Mormons began leaving their temporary refuge in Nebraska in the spring of 1846. They headed west, toward the sanctuary of the Rocky Mountains. This was the great Mormon migration, and most of the time the Mormons walked. Sometimes they had cattle, oxen to pull wagons, and then they would ride some of the time on the wagons. Later, after several groups had taken off, all the Mormon cattle were gone from Nebraska, already gone to Utah. So Brigham Young, originally a carpenter, came up with the idea of the carts. Sort of like wheelbarrows with two wooden wheels and enough of a platform to hold the worldly possessions of one person, the person whose task it was to wheel that cart by hand and foot across the breadth of America, from Nebraska to Utah.

Many of those persons were women, Mormon women, remarkable Mormon women. Ursulia Hascall, mother of Irene Hascall Pomeroy, mother-in-law of Francis Pomeroy, grandmother of young Thales Pomeroy, kept a journal. While quoting from that journal, Wallace Stegner comments on Ursulia, on the spirit he found in her heart: "She had a knack for making the best of things. If it had hailed stones big as baseballs she would have come out from shelter wondering if it wasn't a good time to make up a nice freezer of ice cream."

Francis Pomeroy, her son-in-law, must have wanted to murder her, probably about a thousand times. It is easy to be irritated with a woman like that, a person like that, but of course you have to love her, and I do, but what I like most about that passage is Stegner's wry description. He makes Ursulia sound remarkable, and Margaret Dalglish is more remarkable still.

How the Cat Clan Reduced from Six to Three

First there were seven. Max got mixed up with a dolly, and then there were six, Dudley, Blackie, Polkadot, Happy, Monkey, and Delores, the mom.

Dudley, thin, lithe, more white than gray, Melanie's cat, ran into the road,…just as Pepper had years ago—a family, a city, a state ago. I heard howling and spitting from the front yard of the house in Houston, on Bissonnet, a busy street, near Rice University. Pepper was protecting the family, challenging an intruder cat. When I distracted them by opening the door, the intruder cat took off into the street, and Pepper took off right on her tail.

A truck just missed the intruder cat but hit Pepper. She rolled under the truck, tumbled over and over, came up running back into our yard, down the side of the house, and away. I searched the yard, peered under bushes, but could not find the body.

Four or five days later, eating dinner in the kitchen, we heard meowing coming from the backyard. Pepper was on the roof of the house, not as good as ever, but....

Dudley was crushed by a car on the road, Hilltown Road, directly in front of the Pond House. Melanie asked me to help her make a cross. We painted it white and wrote Dudley's name on it. Melanie decorated it with flower stickers, and we stuck it in the ground over Dudley's grave.

Blackie's death remains a mystery. Sheila was up early on a Sunday morning, doing laundry. When she finished the first load, she took it out back to hang up and saw Blackie lying dead on the grass, under the clotheslines. Except for not breathing, she looked fine.

I spotted the corpse of Polkers on the road one morning on my way to work, halfway down the hill to the east of the Pond House. Polkadot, Crystal's cat. All three of them are buried down in the woods, not far from the creek.

By late spring of 2001, only three cats were left, two of the kittens and one Delores. Two young cats and one grown cat, with three cat rules for staying alive at the Pond House.

The first cat rule for staying alive is Happy's rule. Look both ways before crossing Hilltown Road. The barns are over there, across the road, full of mice. Happy travels safely and forth, forth and back, always looking both ways.

The second cat rule for staying alive is Monkey's rule. Never leave the house. Be afraid of everything. Stay always in Chuckie's room and hide whenever you hear a strange noise.

The third cat rule for staying alive is Delores's rule. Never cross the road. Hang out by the pond. Watch the frogs hop and swim, the turtles bask in the sun. Wander into the woods occasionally. Run away when new kittens are born and come back when they go away. Lie down on my chest and help me write these stories.

Margaret Dalglish

The Mormons migrated in 1846, 1847, all the way into the

eighteen-fifties. They are still migrating today. To Utah. From Nebraska and England and the Slavic Nations. From everywhere. The Church of Jesus Christ of Latter-day Saints is the fastest growing religion in the world.

Margaret Dalglish made her migration in 1856, late in the year, one of the last years of the great migration, a long year of many migrating groups, parties, companies, companies of Mormons. One arrived on November ninth, but, again in the words of Wallace Stegner:

> Until the last of November others were straggling in, most riding in wagons, a few still grimly hauling their battered carts, still defiantly on their own legs. Margaret Dalglish of the Martin company, a gaunt image of Scottish fortitude, dragged her handful of belongings to the very rim of the valley, but when she looked down and saw the end of it she did something extraordinary. She tugged the cart over to the edge of the road and gave it a push and watched it roll and crash and burst apart, scattering into Emigration Canyon the last things she owned on earth. Then she went on into Salt Lake to start the new life with nothing but her gaunt bones, her empty hands, and her stout heart.

I love Margaret Dalglish. I might have married her, taken her as one of my serial wives. She did exactly what *I* would have done, the character I call *I*, if *I* had pushed a frickin' cart across the breadth of America, over the mountains and through the woods and across the desert sands and through all the goddamn rivers.

The Most Incredible One

Yes, the Mormon women were incredible. Ursulia Hascall was incredible. Margaret Dalglish was incredible. But none was more incredible than John Doyle Lee's most notable wife, Emma Batchelor Lee.

The Miracle Kitten

They multiply, it seems, whether you want them to or not. How many cats is enough cats? As many cats as a person wants? As many cats as want that person, that clan of persons?

We started with what? Seven cats? A mom cat and six kitten cats, imported from Salt Lake City, from the Kingdom of Moroni. Four died, tragically, breaking a bunch of family hearts, four of the kittens, two-thirds of the younger generation, Max, Blackie, Polkadot, and Dudley. Everybody grieved, some more so than others, except for the cats that survived. They seemed not to notice the deaths of their brothers, their sisters, their daughters and sons.

And then began the re-multiplication, the re-increase-igation, of the cat population. Crystal was down by the pond one day, Crystalline Crystal, playing with spiders or gigging some frogs, when Misty showed up, rubbing her thick fur on Crystal's left leg. A mystery kitten from nowhere, sort of striped, mostly gray with black hairs, white hairs, a slight red shadow throughout. Unbelievably soft fur. I claimed her, the family undertaker of cats, the guy with the shovel.

And the barn had cats, the barn across the road, Hilltown Road, the barn that long ago was part of the Pond House Farm, back before the subdividing of the land. Orange-colored tabby cats, like Ginger, who crossed the road one day and joined the clan. Later, one we came to call Mom Cat began hanging around, a sickly cat and loose in her morals, unmarried as far as anyone could tell, but suddenly pregnant.

All but one of those kittens died shortly after birth, and the survivor has been sick ever since. But she lived, this sick cat, became Mom Cat II when she had a litter of her own, a tiny litter of three, the three creatures that caused the mental breakdown and self-exile of Delores, the mother of the original cat clan.

Melanie claimed the first of this brood and named it Gucci, a medium red tabby just like her mom—Gucci's mom, though Sheila has red hair too. Crystal claimed the middle kitten, the plump one lighter red in color, and named it Tubbs. Chuckie got the baby, the white one, the one the girls thought might be albino, and named it Albi, Albi the Albino.

They survived, grew, learned to wrestle with one another, became lively enough to scare the bejesus out of Delores, who moved to the garage as has been told.

By then it was September, then the end of September, the twenty-fifth, in the year 2004. I had been replacing windows all summer long. The upstairs windows, all seventeen of them, every window on the second floor of the Pond House. I was working from the front of the house to the back. I started with the three windows in Chuckie's room, then did the one in the hallway, then the three in Crystal's room, then the one in my home office. Eight windows done, almost half the job, by late September.

Now it was the twenty-fifth, a Sunday morning, the sun shining as brilliantly as I was told it was on the day that John Berryman died. I was doing Melanie's windows in assembly line fashion, a destruction and assembly line, first going from old window to old window, removing the stops, removing the sashes upper and lower, going outside and up the ladder to remove the combination storm windows, coming back inside to scrape, clean, patch, level, and shim the frames.

The room was open to the sunshine and the fresh air, seeming brighter and fresher than it had ever been before, when Sheila appeared with her oohs and her ahs, her expressions of pride in her hard-working man. Then Melanie arrived, "What's up, how ya comin', when can I move back in?" Then Tubbs snuck in and began poking around in the stuff on the floor—paint chips, slivers of wood, old nails, dried up caulking—batting the moving pieces, chasing them around the room.

Melanie bent down and picked up Tubbs, but Tubbs resisted, wanted to get back to her adventure down on the floor. Melanie held on tighter, tried clutching Tubbs to her chest, but Tubbs resisted even harder, writhing around, scratching. Melanie began to lose control, struggled harder to hold on, but Tubbs fought harder to get loose, did get loose, did propel herself somehow from Melanie's arms and out through one of those wide open window frames.

"Gasp," said Melanie.

"Oh, my God," said Sheila, and the two of them rushed out the door and down the stairs. I looked out the window, expecting to see snow, railroad tracks, a frozen river, an empty eyeglass case. Tubbs was lying on the bricks of the patio, thrashing frantically from side to side.

By the time I got downstairs and out to the patio, the kitten was dead. Sheila and Melanie were standing there crying. Crystal and Chuckie followed me out the door, asked what happened, joined in the crying.

I felt Tubbs's chest, to see if she was breathing, then felt around her neck for a pulse. "I'm afraid she's dead. You guys might as well go inside."

I walked to the garage, got the shovel, went to the woods, dug a hole, then returned to the patio to retrieve the body. Tubbs gave a little twitch. I bent down and checked again. There may have been a heartbeat, I wasn't sure.

I went in the house and told the mourners that we would give it a little time, keep an eye on the situation. Crystal's cheeks were rivered with tears. "Can I see her?" she asked. Tubbs was Crystal's cat, the middle kitten, the middle girl. She went out to the patio.

"I'm going to stay here with her. Can you get me a blanket?" Someone went upstairs and got a blanket. Crystal wrapped it around Tubbs and sat down on the concrete steps, holding the kitten package in her lap.

The other mourners hung around for a while, supportive, worried, hopeful. I went back up to Melanie's room and started to install the new windows, putting them in, taking them out, making adjustments, going outside and up and down the ladder, coming back in, making gradual progress.

The hours crept by. I brought a pillow for Crystal's back, but she hardly moved all afternoon. Tubbs never more than twitched, the whole afternoon and evening.

In the morning Tubbs was wiggling. Around noon she staggered groggily to the water dish. Along toward evening she ate some food. The next morning she was back on the floor in Crystal's room, wrestling with Gucci and Albi. By Tuesday, the twenty-seventh of September, 2004, she seemed back to normal.

Melanie decided that Tubbs needed a new name. "Miracle," she said. "That's what we will call her. She's the miracle kitten." It did feel that way, like a miracle.

The kitten jumped out the window but did not die.

Part XIII
Polygamy and a Runaway

Goldfinches

2006, May, the seventh. I am out back of the Pond House, laptop on my lap, sitting in my chair under a maple tree, with a view of the pond, a patch of lawn, a meadow, and a bunch of other trees, from one of which hangs a bird feeder, a finch feeder. Today it is mobbed by finches, most of them goldfinches, some of them purple finches, an occasional redpole.

A few minutes ago, all of the birds at the feeder were goldfinches, boys and girls, mothers and fathers, males and females. It felt like some kind of miracle, that conflagration of goldfinches, the dramatic finches, the beautiful ones. "Gold" is a misnomer, a misnomer or a metaphor. American goldfinches are not gold in color. They are a startling shade of yellow, with black markings on their wings, tails, and foreheads. Gold, the precious metal, seven hundred dollars an ounce and more.

Looking at that conflagration of goldfinches, I thought to myself, they must be related to one another, all of them, probably siblings or cousins, maybe offspring and moms and dads. How could they not be?

Is this a result of polygamy? Of the old-time monogamy? Of my brand of monogamy, the kind I call serial matrimonial monogamy? *Marriage?* cheep the goldfinches in a chorus of one. *What's marriage?*

The Notion of Distractions, the Notion of a Thesis

That was a distraction. I sat down to revise, was distracted by the goldfinches, and ended up writing something new. Distractions are always a problem. Distractions are an aspect of the project, of the structure of the sections and parts, the ongoing project of the book. The ongoing project of the family, my family, the Pond House family, the family that so distracts me—distracts me from the Mormon notion of family, which is another part of the book, the ongoing history of the Mormon notion of family, of community.

In the Mormon sections in this Part, I am going to present Mormon polygamy through a series of James Ellroyan document inserts. Quotations. From documents that talk about Mormon polygamy. The quotations will come in bunches, in alternate sections.

After the first two, that is, the two quotations in this section, the ones that might be my thesis about the notion of family. Don't expect much. The thesis is as loose and oblique as a thesis can be. But it is as much of a thesis as I am comfortable having. I give you my first document insert:

> In spite of the ideal of selfless love and devotion to God's commands, polygamous life strained the Saints in geometric proportions as the number of wives and children increased.
> —Thomas G. Alexander

The thesis applies to polygamy, Mormon polygamy. The thesis applies to serial matrimonial monogamy, my version of serial matrimonial monogamy. The thesis applies to the stepdaughters, the three girls adopted by Sheila and Sean, during Sheila's marriage to Sean. Their adoptive daughters, my stepdaughters, the thing about being the stepfather to another three children, about being merely the stepfather, a kind of interloper with few if any rights, about I, I and the character I call *I*—I, who "speak the words of my love: / I, with no rights in this matter, / Neither father nor lover," with only my hungry heart. The lines are from Theodore Roethke's "Elegy for Jane / *My Student, Thrown by a Horse*."

Midnight in the Home of a Bishop

Mormon Polygamy:
Basic Information: A Collection of Document Inserts

It was in Kirtland…that Joseph began to tamper delicately
with one of the most basic mores in Occidental society.
He looked upon that society with the singular detachment
that can come only to a man satisfied with his own ultimate
authority and possessed by a longing to remold the world
closer to his heart's desire. Nothing was so sacred that it
could not be recast into a new utility or a new beauty.

Monogamy seemed to him—as it has seemed to many
men who have not ceased to love their wives, but who have
grown weary of connubial exclusiveness—an intolerably
circumscribed way of life…. But Joseph was no careless
libertine who could be content with clandestine mistresses.
There was too much of the Puritan in him, and he could not
rest until he had redefined the nature of sin and erected a
stupendous theological edifice to support his new theories
on marriage.

Joseph was not given to self-searching or he might have
been troubled by the intensity of his preoccupation with
the nature of adultery. But when he described the new patriarchal order of marriage to Parley Pratt during their weeks
together in Philadelphia in 1840, it was with the freshness
and enthusiasm of a man who had stumbled quite by chance
upon an ancient treasure….

Pratt had buried his first wife, with whom he had been
very much in love, and had since remarried. Joseph now
promised him that he would have both wives in heaven
provided that he was sealed to them in the temple under
the new and everlasting covenant. And since heaven would
bless his union with both wives in the hereafter, it could no
logically frown on his having more than one wife on earth

There was plenty of precedent for plural marriages in the
Old Testament, beginning with Father Abraham. But it wa

Jacob's polygamous marriages that particularly interested Joseph Smith, and he frequently referred to the new marriage principle as the blessing of Jacob. He was fond of pointing to the commandment in Exodus: "And if a man should entice a maid that is not betrothed, and lie with her, he shall surely endow her to be his wife." The sin of adultery lay not in the act itself but in the subsequent desertion....

Joseph taught none of this openly, for he feared that polygamy would bring down the wrath of the gentiles. Until the day it could be publicly proclaimed, any whisper of the doctrine of plural wives must be vehemently denied, and any man caught preaching it without his own personal sanction must be summarily cut off from the church.

—Fawn M. Brodie

Polygamous families represented the elite of Mormon communities. These were bishops, stake presidents, and high councilmen—successful businessmen, professionals, and farmers and their multiple wives.... In many cases, church leaders refused to ordain men to administrative callings unless they took an additional wife.

—Thomas G. Alexander

If a man went to heaven with ten wives, he would have more than tenfold the blessings of a mere monogamist, for all the children begotten through these wives would enhance his kingdom. The man with only one wife, on the other hand, would be denied even her and forced to spend eternity as a ministering angel rather than a god.

—Fawn M. Brodie

Black Wednesday

2005, January. I am in Charlotte teaching people how to write at the weeklong, low-residency MFA program January residency.

A long week of workshops, seminars, conferences, readings, presentations.

Wednesday is my day off. I read submitted manuscripts and prepare the all-program seminar I must deliver later in the week. In the late afternoon I get in the car and head for Shelby, Shelby, North Carolina, thirty-five miles west of Charlotte. I am going to spend the evening with Jon, one of my sons, and Allison and Tristan, two of my grandchildren.

I am on the road when my cell phone rings. "Melanie is gone," says Sheila. "She ran away again. I don't know what to do."

"What happened? Where are you?"

"In town, at the school, a basketball game. Crystal is playing. Rebekkah is selling popcorn. And Melanie is gone."

"Why? Why did she run?"

"I swear I did not yell or anything. She took my cell phone, had put an old one in my purse to fool me. I tried to use it and it didn't work. I got mad at her, but I didn't even raise my voice! I swear! There are people everywhere here. She just ran off!"

Oh, Jesus, I think. To Sheila I say, "Not again."

"I have to go," says Sheila. "I have to find her. I will call you later."

I continue on toward Shelby. Night continues to fall.

Mormon Polygamy:
The Fictitious Side: A Long Document Insert

The Mormon seraglio is very strictly and systematically organized. It forms a grand lodge, as it were, and is divided into three distinct orders or degrees. The first and lowest of these is styled the *"Cyprian Saints"*; the second, the *"Chambered Sisters of Charity"*; and the third and highest degree is called the *"Cloistered Saints,"* or *"Consecratees of the Cloister."*…

THE CYPRIAN SAINTS

The members of the Female Relief Society, who are ever on the watch for victims, have the power, when they know or even suspect, that any Mormon female has, however slightly, lapsed from the straight path of virtue, without the sanction or knowledge of the Prophet, of bringing her at once before the Inquisition.... [T]he poor, terrified female is questioned and threatened, until she confesses the crime she has committed, or perhaps, in her confusion and terror, accuses herself of what she was never guilty of. She is immediately, by the council, pronounced a Cyprian.... She takes the *White Veil*, and her name and failing are stealthily promulgated among the *trustworthy* members of the Church, at whose command she is, for licentious purposes, forever after. [The Cyprians are] a class set apart and appropriated to the gratification of the vilest appetites of the brutal Priests and Elders of the Mormon Church....

THE CHAMBERED SISTERS OF CHARITY

This order comprises that class of females who indulge their sensual propensities, without restraint, whether married or single, by the express permission of the Prophet.

Whenever one of the "Saints"...of the male sex, becomes enamored of a female, and she responds to the feeling by a reciprocal manifestation, the loving brother goes to Holy Joe, and states the case. It makes, by the bye, no difference whatever if one or both the parties are already provided with conjugal helpmates. The Prophet gravely buries his face in his hat, in which lies his peep-stone, and inquires of the Lord what are his will and pleasure in the matter. Sometimes, when Joe wants the woman for his own purposes, an unfavorable answer is given; but, generally, the reply permits the parties to follow the bent of their inclinations, which they do without further ceremony....

Thus these poor, deluded females,...incited...to indulgence in the most degrading passions, have their consciences soothed, and their scruples appeased, by the sanction of the pretended Apostle and Prophet of the Lord, in whom they have the utmost confidence, and whose lightest word is with them a law.

The result of this system is, that not infrequently men having wives of their own are living in licentious intercourse with other women, and not infrequently with other men's wives; thus multiplying their adulteries, and producing an incalculable amount of domestic discord and misery. . .

The *Chambered Sisters of Charity* are… "*Saints of the Green Veil,*" and are by no means niggardly of their favors to any of the faithful. Provided the Holy Joe does not desire to monopolize any of them, they are at the service of each and all of the apostles, High Priests, and Elders of Israel…

THE CONSECRATEES OF THE CLOISTER, OR CLOISTERED SAINTS

This degree is composed of females, whether married or unmarried, who, by an express grant and gift of God, through his Prophet the Holy Joe, are set apart and consecrated to the use and benefit of particular individuals, as *secret, spiritual wives.* They are the *Saints of the Black Veil,* and are accounted the special favorites of Heaven…. Their spiritual husbands are altogether from the most eminent members of the Mormon Church, and participate in the holiness of their consecrated wives….

This is the highest degree in the Harem, and, in the order of the Prophet's licentious arrangements, is held as the very acme of perfection, and it is, indeed, the *ne plus ultra* of depravity…. It is no obstacle whatever to this spiritual marriage if one or both of the parties should happen to have a husband or wife, already united to them according to the laws of the land….

The above is a faithful and unexaggerated account of the most enormous and detestable system of depravity that was ever concocted by the corrupt heart of a human being

—Apostate John Cook Bennett, *The History of the Saint*

An Evening in Shelby, North Carolina

The barbecue has been eaten, coleslaw and potato salad, and now we are drinking home-brewed stout and Jon is demonstrating his new high-definition TV. Tristan and Allison are running around the house, playing some crazy game.

My cell phone rings. "I have looked everywhere," says Sheila. "I have called all her friends. No one knows where she is. Angie is out looking. Shawn is looking. Should I call the police?"

I wonder, *Shawn? Angie?* Oh, Melanie's former boyfriend and his mother. "I don't know about calling the police," I say. "What time is it? Seven thirty? Maybe give it another hour."

"But this is the town," says Sheila. "It isn't like when she runs away at home, in the country. Here she could be in trouble."

"Keep looking. Keep calling me."

I meet Frannie, the new dog. Allison has studied Frannie's habits, her personality, her character, and she explains these things to me. Frannie is a wiener dog, not much fur but lots of soft skin; skittish, running endlessly around the yard, looking for a means of escape. Allison is a girl, nine years old. Her first name is my middle name.

I head back to Charlotte, to the Doubletree Suites, after promising to return on Saturday, after graduation, when the residency is over. We can spend some more time together, the family. Family is everything.

Mormon Polygamy:
The Light Side: A Collection of Document Inserts

> The men who were taken into the system [of polygamy] at this early period—Hyrum Smith, Brigham Young, Heber Kimball, William Clayton, Willard Richards, and Benjamin F. Johnson—after an initial period of shock and spiritual torment, were won over with very little argument.
> —Fawn M. Brodie

At a private meeting on May 5, 1842, Joseph explained

the principle [of polygamy] to Brigham Young and Heber C. Kimball, who had just returned from missions to England. Within six weeks, after much hesitation, both had taken plural wives....

[In 1846] Brigham Young brought seventeen wives out of Nauvoo, John D. Lee had ten, George A. Smith six, and Heber C. Kimball listed thirty-two.

— Juanita Brooks, *John Doyle Lee*

Polygamy promised renewed youth. During the reformation in 1857, Heber C. Kimball declared that God would shower his grace on those who entered polygamy. "I have noticed," he said, "that a man who has but one wife, and is inclined to that doctrine, soon begins to wither and dry up, while a man who goes into plurality looks fresh, young, and sprightly. Why is this? Because God loves that man, and because he honors His work and word."

— Thomas G. Alexander

Critics [of polygamy] had the force of reputable science on their side. Relying in part on nineteenth-century assumptions about the effect of lifestyle on genetic inheritance and in part on what they said was first-hand observation, Dr. Samuel A. Cartwright and Professor C. G. Forshey at the New Orleans Academy of Sciences in 1861 argued that intercourse among one man and multiple wives begat genetic deviants who resembled crosses between Neanderthals and Frankenstein's monster. Cartwright and Forshey descried in the offspring of polygamy the "yellow, sunken, cadaverous visage," "greenish-colored" eyes, "thick, protuberant lips," "low" foreheads, "light, yellowish hair," and "lank angular" frames.

— Thomas G. Alexander

The Police Get Involved

When I call Sheila while driving back to Charlotte, she says she is still looking for Melanie. Now the police are involved, knocking on the doors of Melanie's friends, her in-town friends, questioning the kids and the parents.

Later, as I pace the floor in my room while scratching my head, the cell phone rings. "They found her," Sheila says. "She was in a closet at some kid's house. I have to go to the police station. I will call you later."

I lie in bed, try to read a book, turn the TV on and off, waiting for the phone to ring. At eleven thirty, I finally call Sheila. She does not answer. At twelve thirty my cell phone rings.

"She is here," Sheila says. They have her in a room at the police station. She fought with the officer when he tried to get her out of the closet. She scratched his arms and bit his hands. He had to handcuff her. She will not talk to me."

I worry about Crystal and Rebekkah. "Where are the other kids?"

"They are here with me," Sheila says. "She won't talk to them either. The police are calling Children's Services. I don't know what will happen. I have to go."

"Oh, Jesus," I say. "Call me as soon as you can.

Mormon Polygamy:
The Dark Side: A Collection of Document Inserts

The most deadly sin among the [Mormon] people was adultery, and many men were killed in Utah for that reason.
— John Doyle Lee

[Mormonism] enforces the systematic degradation of women, not only permits but orders, the commission of the vilest lusts, in the name of Almighty God himself, and teaches that it is a sacred duty to commit the crimes of theft and murder.

— Judge Cradlebaugh

In Utah [castration] was the favorite revenge of old, worn out members of the Priesthood, who wanted young women

sealed to them, and found that the girl preferred some handsome young man. The old Priests generally got the girls,
and many a young man was unsexed for refusing to give up
his sweetheart at the request of an old and failing, but still
sensual apostle or member of the Priesthood.

— John Doyle Lee

The Decision

At one o'clock, maybe one thirty, my cell phone rings again.

"Melanie still won't talk to me," says Sheila. "She won't go home
with me. The women from Children's Services think the best thing
is to take her to Abraxis."

"Abraxis?," I ask. "What is Abraxis?"

"It's a facility. Detention. Incarceration. She will be safe there.
She will get therapy. It's tightly run, lots of discipline," Sheila says.
Then, almost sobbing, "Oh, God! My baby!"

"What do you think?" I ask. "What do the police think?"

"They agree with the women," Sheila says. "I don't know what
to do. Maybe it's the best thing. What do you think?"

"I don't know either. Maybe it is the best thing. She's got to learn."

Sheila decides. Melanie will go to Abraxis. When Melanie gets
wind of the decision, she has a sudden change of heart. Now she
is eager to go home with Sheila.

Sheila says, "No." Melanie is going to Abraxis. Rebekkah hears
this and goes ballistic. Chuckie Walker shoves Sheila, cries, and
runs from the room.

My heart flutters when I hear these things. *Oh, Jesus.*

Mormon Polygamy:
The Darkest Side: A Long Document Insert

Warren Snow was Bishop of the Church at Manti, San
Pete County, Utah. He had several wives, but there was a
fair, buxom young woman in the town that Snow wanted

for a wife. He made love to her with all his powers, went to parties where she was, visited her at her home, and proposed to make her his wife. She thanked him for the honor offered, but told him she was then engaged to a young man, a member of the Church, and consequently could not marry the old priest. This was no sufficient reason to Snow. He told her it was the will of God that she should marry him, and she must do so; that the young man could be got rid of, sent on a mission or dealt with in some way so as to release her from her engagement—that, in fact, a promise made to the young man was not binding, when she was informed that it was contrary to the wishes of the authorities.

The girl continued obstinate. The "teachers" of the town visited her and advised her to marry Bishop Snow. Her parents, under the orders of the counselor of the Bishop, also insisted that their daughter must marry the old man. She still refused. Then the authorities called on the young man and directed him to give up the young woman. This he steadfastly refused to do. He was promised Church preferment, celestial rewards, and everything that could be thought of—all to no purpose. He remained true to his intended, and said he would die before he would surrender his intended wife to the embraces of another.

This *unusual* resistance of authority by the young people made Snow more anxious than ever to capture the girl. The young man was ordered to go on a mission to some distant locality, so that the authorities would have no trouble in effecting their purpose of forcing the girl to marry as they desired. But the mission was refused by the still contrary and unfaithful young man.

It was then determined that the rebellious young man must be forced by harsh treatment to respect the advice and orders of the Priesthood. His fate was left to Bishop Snow for his decision. He decided that the young man should be castrated; Snow saying, "When that is done, he will not be liable to want the girl badly, and she will listen to reason when she knows that her lover is no longer a man."

It was then decided to call a meeting of the people who lived true to counsel, which was to be held in the schoolhouse in Manti, at which place the young man should be present, and dealt with according to Snow's will. The meeting was called. The young man was there, and was again requested, ordered and threatened, to get him to surrender the young woman to Snow, but true to his plighted troth, he refused to consent to give up the girl. The lights were then put out. An attack was made on the young man. He was severely beaten, and then tied with his back down on a bench, when Bishop Snow took a bowie-knife, and performed the operation in a most brutal manner, and then took the portion severed from his victim and hung it up in the schoolhouse on a nail, so that it could be seen by all who visited the house afterwards....

After this outrage old Bishop Snow took occasion to get up a meeting at the schoolhouse, so as to get the people of Manti, and the younger woman that he wanted to marry, to attend the meeting. When all had assembled, the old man talked to the people about their duty to the Church, and their duty to obey counsel, and the dangers of refusal, and then publicly called attention to the mangled parts of the young man, that had been severed from his person, and stated that the deed had been done to teach the people that the counsel of the Priesthood must be obeyed. To make a long story short, I will say, the young woman was soon after forced into being sealed to Bishop Snow.

Brigham Young, when he heard of this treatment of the young man, was very mad, but did nothing against Snow. He left him in charge as Bishop at Manti, and ordered the matter to be hushed up. This is only one instance of many that I might give to show the danger of refusing to obey counsel in Utah.

— John Doyle Lee

Chuckie Walker

Now it is Saturday morning. I am in my room, finishing the preparation for my all-program seminar on editing, on what to expect after the MFA if you get a job in editing.

Things have been quiet at home since Melanie was taken to Abraxis by Children Services, relatively quiet. Rebekkah is still upset, worried about her sister. Crystal thinks it is for the best, thinks Melanie needs settling down. Sheila is coping.

My cell phone rings. "God," says Sheila, "you won't believe this."

"What did she do now?" I ask. Melanie is in detention, beginning to learn her lesson. I wonder what she could have done.

"Nothing," says Sheila. "It isn't Melanie. It's Rebekkah." Chuckie was spending last night at Jenna's house. "She started throwing up at two a.m. and never stopped," Sheila says. "I had to take her to the ER."

"Sweet Jesus. What did they say?"

"They couldn't find anything wrong. They sent us back home, said to keep an eye on things, and if she doesn't get better, bring her back."

"How is she now?" Nine in the morning, maybe ten.

"Better," says Sheila. "She's still sleeping. She hasn't vomited for a while."

We talk about Melanie. Abraxis has strict rules. She is allowed two phone calls home a week and one visit from the family. She has the right to refuse both these things, the phone calls and the visits. For now she is saying no, being defiant.

Crystal is doing fine—still angry with Melanie, but keeping an eye on Chuckie and maintaining the order in her own life. Bringing some order to the house. Her room a mess as usual, but her life is orderly.

The seminar is at one, my two-hour seminar. My last workshop is at three, graduation is at five. By six, six thirty at the latest, I can be back on the road to Shelby. A bottle of home-brewed stout. Some family time. I worry about Chuckie Walker. The operation was almost eight months ago, in May 2004, her appendectomy.

At twelve thirty Sheila calls again. Chuckie is up, pale and wan. Weak. Not interested in food.

At two forty-five I am on my break between the seminar and the workshop, drinking a cup of coffee. Sheila calls. Chuckie is awake but just lying there, on the couch, not even petting the dog. She has no appetite.

The workshop goes well. This is going to be a good semester. Three talented writers, hard workers, experts in spelling and punctuation, unlikely to split infinitives and dangle modifiers.

Graduation is graduation. The codirectors both speak—go forth and write, come back and visit, drive safely, we love you and will miss you. A vice president of the college speaks—we love having the program here, you are all wonderful, and the faculty!, unbelievable!, superstars, all of them! The students accept their diplomas, give surprise gifts to the codirectors. It happens every semester.

I say my goodbyes. Six o'clock in the January evening, maybe six thirty. I hug a lot of people, look forward to seeing them again and again, get in the car and head for Shelby, ready to relax. I plan to stay overnight and drive home to Gettysburg in the morning.

I call home from the car, but no one answers. I try Sheila's cell phone, but no one answers. I am maybe fifteen miles down the road toward Shelby when Crystal finally picks up the home phone. "Let me talk to Mom," I say.

"She isn't here," says Crystal. "She took Rebekkah back to the hospital. She started vomiting again."

I call the emergency room. They find Sheila. Chuckie Walker has a blockage in her upper intestine, scar tissue. She is scheduled for surgery.

I turn the car around, phone my regrets to Jon, drive all night.

Part XIV
Emma and Sheila

In the Hands of the State

Melanie had no fun in Abraxis. She had to wear institutional clothes, walk in a line, make her bed, say "Yes, sir" and "No, sir" and "Yes, ma'am" and "No, ma'am." She had to follow all the rules or else.

We could take her out at any time within the next month, out of Abraxis. If she stayed more than a month, her future would pass into the hands of the system, which then would decide her fate. We had had enough of that. Melanie for sure had. Before she was adopted by Sheila and Sean, she had been a ward of the state of New Mexico. A little bit of being a ward of the state goes a long way.

We took her home just before the end of the month, the month of order, discipline, no talking back. No hiding and no running away. No wasting time on the phone. One phone call a week, to her parents only, five minutes, no longer, one visit a week, but only if she wanted it. We could not force ourselves on her. Who knew? Maybe her problem was the family. Maybe she just needed space from us, maybe that was why she was running away. For sure we needed space from her.

Once she was out, we were required to start therapy, again, family therapy. Putting her in Abraxis meant working with the system. Now we had to work with the county, with Children's Services. We began family therapy. Everyone had to go. We are still going. We were there today.

Emma and the Navajos:
A Commentary with a Document Insert

Sheila's putting Melanie in Abraxis was tough, a case of tough love. Tough for Sheila and tough for Melanie. Sheila wanted to make the best choice for Melanie. Sometimes the best choice is to do the toughest thing.

Emma did something like that, Emma Lee, John Doyle Lee's most incredible wife. Emma Lee protected her children through a kind of tough love, tough on her, tough on the children, tough on the Indians. John Doyle Lee was in prison, awaiting his conviction, his execution. Emma was at their home, at Lonely Dell, in Arizona, on the Colorado River, where Lee had established his ferry. The very place where, today, if you take a rafting trip through the Grand Canyon, you may board your raft.

Lonely Dell was a lonely place back then, in the day of Emma. The Indians were always a threat, especially to a lone white woman, a lone white woman and her children in the middle of nowhere. Here is what Emma did when threatened by the Indians, alone at Lonely Dell, in the words of Juanita Brooks, John Doyle Lee's biographer:

> Word had gone out of Lee's capture, so that even the Indians knew. One night soon after, a band of Navajos crossed the river and camped at the clearing not far from Emma's house, but contrary to their usual custom, they did not come up to trade or ask for food.... Emma...sensed a difference in their actions...her mind ran...to knifings and scalpings until she was almost petrified with fear.
>
> As night fell and she could see the Indian campfire glowing in the darkness, the braves standing and moving about as though restless and waiting, she became desperate. What should she do?... She prayed earnestly for guidance and inspiration...and asked for God's protecting hand to be over them. As she arose, she had her answer.

Instead of locking the house securely as she had intended to do, she told the children that they were going out to sleep at the Indian camp that night. She loaded Billy and Ike with quilts, gave Jimmie and Belle and each of the twins a pillow, and told them to follow her, youngest first. She picked up the tiny baby in her arms, and leading little 2-year-old Dellie by the hand, guided the procession, past the corrals, along the trail through the scrub brush, to the clearing.

The chief, surprised, turned to meet them.

"I am afraid, very much afraid," she told him in her combination of Navajo and English and pantomime. "See all my papooses. Yawgett's [John Doyle Lee's] papooses. They are afraid, too. You are a big, brave chief. You are Yawgett's friend. You will watch my papooses so they not be hurt during the dark hours. Let me make my bed down here, close to your camp, so that you can watch over my tiny papooses."

The chief was moved by her appeal. Pointing to a smooth place in the clearing, he motioned the boys to make the bed there....

[Emma] had planned to keep her vigil all night, but... fell asleep. When she roused it was broad daylight. She remembered where she was, listened a minute to the quiet breathing of the children in the stillness, and raised up to look around. The Indians were gone! Down the trail as it wound over the hill she saw them pass single file on their way to Kanab.

The chief told the incident to Jacob Hamblin at Kanab, with the word that Emma was a "heap brave squaw."

Emma Lee, my favorite of Lee's many wives, a brave, tough woman. And Sheila, my third wife, a brave, tough, and loving woman. It was tough love, what she did, sending Melanie to Abraxis, the eldest of her adopted daughters. Protecting the family, making the best decision, breaking her own heart in the process, her husband away.

Sheila's Bag of Carrots

Tuesday, September 20, 2005. Another hour with the family therapist, the usual back and forth, everyone getting their chance to talk, the focus as always mostly on Melanie, mostly on Melanie and Sheila, their relationship.

We have a routine. Sheila picks the kids up at school at the end of their day. I drive over from work. Sheila brings something for the kids to eat, a snack, something healthy. Today she brought a bag of baby carrots. The kids were munching carrots in the waiting room when I arrived.

The session started out tense, got tenser. Melanie was after Sheila's throat, reciting Sheila's errors, Sheila's sins and deficiencies, using the words *always* and *never*. "She never lets me do anything, never lets me go anywhere, never lets me use the Internet. She is always yelling, always griping, always complaining, always saying *no*." Sheila is a bitch in Melanie's eyes, a bitch from hell.

I could feel Sheila steaming beside me in her chair, squirming, seething, beginning to groan through her teeth, a furious, rising, wailing groan. She stood up, said "I am sick of this abuse," took a step toward the door, remembered her purse, turned back to pick it up, stepped again toward the door, thought of something else, turned back, sat down, opened the purse and rummaged around, pulled out the bag of carrots, set it on the floor, and took off again, this time for good.

The therapist glanced at me, his eyebrows raised. "I guess she wanted us to have the carrots," I said.

The therapist looked again at me, then turned to Melanie. "Melanie," he said, "what do you think of your mother leaving?"

The four of us talked about Sheila, Sheila and Melanie, how they get on each other's nerves. The therapist helped us decide that maybe we could help them work that out next week, when we will all be back together again.

It is helpful. The family therapy is irritating, stressful, demeaning, obnoxious, challenging, time consuming, and altogether yucky

Sheila and Melanie in the Photo Booth

but helpful.

Melanie is doing better. She no longer runs away. She stays with us and tries to work things out. Sometimes she acts like a grownup. Sometimes she acts and talks like a thirty-four-year-old woman. A mom. Mostly she is a kid, the adolescent, the obnoxious teenager.

Sheila is Sheila, a make-it-up-as-you-go-along mom. She does what seems right at the time. She has a huge heart. She loves these strangers, these kids birthed by others. She adopted them, assumed that tripartite burden! She cares about them, worries about them, wants them to be healthy, to eat well. That is why she left that bag of carrots behind when she stormed out of the therapy room, that and her innate streak of sweet nuttiness.

We are working things out. We love each other. We are a family. No one said it would be easy. It isn't easy. Adopted kids, then two divorces, a new family—new state, new school, new house, new friends—several dead cats. A new stepfather. None of it is easy, but we are working it out.

Ann Chatterly MacFarlane

Many white settlers were eager to purchase Indian children, in the Kingdom of Moroni, in the nineteenth century, on the American frontier. Because they had no children of their own, because they wanted to raise a child, a servant, or a slave.

Some Indian men were willing to sell whatever Indian children they owned or could seize. A group of the worst Indian braves was known as the Walker band, led by an Indian known as Chief Walker. Here is how one Mormon woman handled the Walker band, down in southern Utah, near Cedar City.

Ann Chatterly MacFarlane "was sewing carpet rags one day when an Indian mother burst into the house, thrust an eighteen-months old baby boy at her, and fled in mortal terror out the back door."

No words were spoken, but Ann knew what was going on. She "picked up her ample petticoats" and hid the child beneath them. The story is from Juanita Brooks's biography of John Doyle Lee:

Three young braves broke into the room. One spoke some English.

"Where papoose?" he asked. "Papoose here. Show where."

"No sabe." Ann looked him straight in the eye and shook her head. Instantly one was on his knees under the bed, while another lifted the lid of the trunk.

The half attic over the bed, the bottom of the cupboard, the wood box beside the stove all were searched, while Ann stood calmly or moved a few steps to keep out of their way. She could feel the baby's two arms tight around her leg as, quiet as a quail, he waited out his fate.

Soon the leader began to talk in a loud, angry tone and to brandish his club. Still Ann did not flinch, but walking [deliberately] to the back door, pointed to the willows along the creek, in the direction opposite to the one in which the mother had gone.

Not until the next night, after the Walker band had moved on, did the Indian mother return for her baby.

I have told you the Mormon women were incredible. Wallace Stegner has told you: "Their women were incredible."

Sheila's Heart

Today is Friday, September 23, 2005. I am out back of the Pond House, under a tree not far from the pond, writing and revising. Every now and then I think about Hurricane Rita, which today is bearing down on southeastern Texas. I think about Pete, my son in Houston, about Janine, about their three children, my grandchildren. I think about Margaret in Port Arthur, Jean's mother, my former mother-in-law.

But mostly I am thinking about Sheila, about the incredible thing she did ten years ago, when she was married to Sean and they were living in Albuquerque, New Mexico. Sheila's dream was to adopt a child, not an easy process: applications, interviews, background checks, a lot of waiting and uncertainty, a lot of fear, then the years on probation while foster parenting, the day in court, a decision good or bad.

After the first steps, the application phase, months went by. Nothing but silence from the state agency. Then one day the phone rang in Sheila's office. Three girls needed a home, half sisters, one mother but three fathers, fathers of identity not certain. A bad situation had suddenly gotten worse, after a history of neglect and abuse. There had been some kind of fight, maybe about drugs, but alcohol was definitely involved.

The mother had gone to a bar downtown, leaving two of the girls—Melanie, the five-year-old, and Rebekkah, the two-year-old—sitting alone on the sidewalk outside. Occasionally the mother would bring Cokes to the girls, as the hours went by. Sometime after midnight she came out with some men and another woman. They walked past the children, walked across the street and into a park. Words were exchanged, charges and counter-charges, threats, and then a fight began. The men and the other woman ganged up on the girls' mother. Melanie took Rebekkah's hand, led her running down the street and into an alley. The police found them there, took them to the station, and turned them over to the state.

Sheila was at work, sitting at her desk, holding the phone to her ear. I can see her with her hand to her mouth. I can hear her saying, "Oh, God." The woman from the state said, "We need to place them. Now. Together if possible. You are our last chance. I know you requested one foster kid, but everyone else is saying no. If you say no, we will have to split them up. The oldest one is five, the others three and two."

Sheila said yes. To keeping the sisters together. Everyone else had said no. She might have said, *You want us to take three kids, not one but three? From a bad background? Unknown fathers? Picked up in an alley by the police in the middle of the night? A drunk mother in a drug deal gone bad? You want us to take these three kids, all at once, now, bam, just like that? You gotta be crazy.*

But Sheila said yes. She looked into her heart, and then she said

"Yes, I will take them."

The social worker said, "Uh…that's wonderful, but your husband has to agree. Call me back after you talk with him."

Sheila called back within the hour: "He said yes. We will take them."

Emma's Midwife

The most incredible of the incredible Mormon women, in my eyes, is Emma Lee. I am going to tell you two more stories. Now. Later I will tell you how she came to be Mrs. Lee.

Near the end of the second year at Lonely Dell, Emma gave birth to her sixth child, maybe her seventh, a girl. John Doyle Lee was stuck in Utah. He had been trying to get back to his river home, but was delayed by the health of a friend. Juanita Brooks:

> Lee knew that Emma would give birth to another baby in early November and wanted desperately to get to her, but everything seemed to conspire against it. Mr. Winterburn became ill from an infected foot, inflamed and painful, and attended by violent chills and fever. Lee could not leave without first doing what he could to ease him. After the crisis seemed past, after he had the crop gathered and stored and sufficient wood cut and stacked against the house, Lee set out…[and] reached the ferry at noon on November 8.
>
> …[Emma] had…a chicken simmering on the back of the stove, with dumplings ready to add to the soup, and steamed squash rings. She took him first to see his little new daughter…[told him about the birth], explained how, when the preliminary pains began, she prepared and laid out everything within reach, how she had the teakettle boiling and the clean squares of cloth heating in the oven for the navel, with scissors close by to cut the cord and string to tie it. She had sent Ike to keep the twins occupied at their playhouse under the tamarack bushes, and to see that little Dell was safe and happy. They were all too young to have

to listen if she cried out toward the last. Nor was Billy to come in until she called him. He was to stay near and say a prayer in his heart for her. When it was over, he must help clear up and bury the afterbirth.

She managed very well except for the last half hour or so.

No one ever said it would be easy. A woman alone at Lonely Dell. Floods and droughts and Indians and temperatures well over one hundred degrees day after day in the summer, blizzards and freezing winds in winter. A ferry boat to operate whenever strangers called, six children to raise alone and care for, and now a seventh to pull safely from her own body.

The Other Cliffhanger

Chuckie was in the hospital, Rebekkah, the daughter I call Chuckie Walker. Scar tissue was blocking her intestines, from the earlier operation, the appendectomy. She had gotten sick in the night and not recovered. Could not eat, could not drink, was in continual pain.

Now she was lying on a gurney, one of those shower caps on her head. Two anesthesiologists stood beside the gurney, conferring. "Yeah," said one, "I did her last time." Last time? Would that the last time had been the last time. Here we were again. It was early in the morning, the morning after my all-night drive home.

This time the operation was quick. No complications. Within an hour Chuckie was in the recovery room. Three or four days later, she was well enough to leave the hospital.

Now she is fine, September 2005, eight months later. Chuckie has put on weight, grown a couple of inches up and out, is taller than her older sisters now.

We had been afraid of losing her. Late-night fears. Sounds kind of silly now, but still. The dark of night is the dark of night.

Here is how Sheila met Chuckie Walker. Met the three kids. The phone call came in the middle of the day, the state of New Mexico with its challenge, decide now, we cannot wait. You cannot see the kids before you decide. Take them or leave them, knowing nothing more than we have told you.

Sheila found Sean. They worked at the same place, but in different buildings. They went for a walk. Sheila was eager to have the children, already committed in her heart. Sean could not turn her down. Maybe he thought about money, about time, time to write and sleep. Maybe he even thought about the adolescent years to come. I don't know. What I do know is what he said. He said, "Yes, if that's what you want, we will take the children."

May I call them saints? Sean and Sheila? The selflessness, how important it was to them that these three sisters not be split apart. May I go overboard and call them saints? Not Mormons, but saints nevertheless.

Emma's Heart

Bad as things were then, they became worse later. What could make things worse? How about a husband in prison, a long trip to see him, a demeaning insult from an insensate moron? Almost exactly a year after the birth of the seventh child, John Doyle Lee was arrested. Juanita Brooks:

> Now began the long period of his confinement. From November 10 until July 23 of the following year, Lee waited for his trial to open. In the meantime he remained cheerful and cooperative, and as [Sheriff] Stokes wrote, "He never gave any trouble to me or his guards. He never tried to escape, but at all times assisted the guards to carry out the instructions they had received from the officers." Because of this he made many friends among the soldiers and officers, and was allowed sometimes to have visitors inside and to come out of doors for a short while each day. Some legends come from this period, one of which is characteristic of Emma.
>
> She had come all the way from Lonely Dell to visit her husband. For the last part of the trip she had borrowed a

buggy and team. Emma was thirty-nine, handsome, well dressed and poised, with a natural ruddy flush in her cheeks. She had carried her buggy whip in her gloved hand, the lash doubled back to the end of the stock. As she came out of the cell through the room where some of the guards were sitting, one man said to another, "Who is that handsome woman?"

"Oh, that is one of John D. Lee's whores," the other answered with a smirk.

In a flash he was struck across the face with the buggy whip, as Emma turned fiercely upon him. Surprised, he ducked to miss the next blow and then turned and ran outside before the third.

No one raised a word or a hand in his defense.

One of Lee's whores. The sex side of polygamy. The other side is the family, the families. The Mormons have always been serious about family, maybe too serious. The early Mormons had many families, many problems, many impediments to solutions; no outside help, no modern conveniences; gratuitous insults galore.

The Gathering of the Clan

They called the state, Sheila and Sean, signed a bunch of papers, were given the address of the foster home where two of the girls were staying, the two who had been rescued by the police. Melanie and Rebekkah were staying at the home of a couple that took care of foster children for shorter or longer periods of time. Opal and Jesse, a white woman and a black man. Perfect for these kids, kids of mixed parentage.

I am telling you Sheila's story, the story Sheila told to me. I came along five years later and missed all this early stuff. What would I have done? The same thing I did five years later. I said yes five years ago, and I am saying it again today. So is Sean. So is Sheila.

They drove out to the house, to Opal and Jesse's house, out beyond the Albuquerque suburbs, out where the country begins. The kind of place where chickens live across the street, across the

The Reunion of Melanie and Crystal

road. Sheila saw Melanie first, from the car. Melanie was standing in the front yard. She had just turned five years old.

"She was Melanie!" Sheila has told me. "A five-year-old version of who she is today—standing there like the president or a general, in charge of all she surveyed, analyzing the situation, measuring the terrain, waiting for an update, ready to take prompt and decisive action." Sheila fell in love at once.

Rebekkah was out back. She wanted to be pushed on the swing. "It was my first bonding experience," Sheila said. "I thought to myself, I can push her on the swing. She will love me. But I pushed too hard, and she fell off the swing and started to cry. I wondered, *How can I ever be a mother? I can't even push a swing!*"

Rebekkah got up, back up on the swing. She has been getting back up ever since.

Then a car pulled up on the road out front. Another social worker had arrived with the third child. Crystal had missed the adventure downtown, the bar, the fight, the police, had been at home with grandpa. Now she was in the car, pulling up at Opal and Jesse's, wondering what was going on. Then she spotted her big sister.

She ran toward Melanie yelling, "My sister!" Melanie ran toward Crystal yelling, "My sister!" Rebekkah and Sheila came from the back yard. "Hi, Cooka," said Rebekkah.

They stood there together, five of them. A new mother, a new father, three sisters, three daughters, a family. It was some kind of miracle.

Part XV
Polygamy and Monogamy

The Good Side of Polygamy

Is there one? A good side to polygamy? Of course: the good side of polygamy is the man's side, the nineteenth-century Mormon man who somehow managed to make it work, a man like John Doyle Lee. Which is not to say that it was easy. And not to say that it was all that good.

John Doyle Lee had nineteen wives—nineteen wives and sixty children. Over time, that is, not all at once. In the Mormon world, wives tended to come and go. Presumably, the longer the marriage and the more children produced, the better the marriage. With seven of his wives, John Doyle Lee had no children. Nine of his marriages lasted fewer than five years and produced a total of three children, one to each of three different wives. The other ten marriages lasted between six and one-half years and thirty-three years, and only one of those was childless.

He married Agatha Ann Woolsey, his first wife, in 1833; she died in 1866 after bearing him eleven children. Between 1846 and 1848 John Doyle Lee accumulated thirteen wives. This was in the early days of Mormon polygamy; lots of men went a little crazy.

Two out of this cluster of marriages lasted thirty-one years, two lasted thirty years, one lasted twelve years, and eight were short-lived. Of Lee's last five wives, whom he married between 1853 and 1865, two produced no children, two produced seven each, and one produced three.

Polygamy was practiced by the elite of Mormon society, the big shots, the bishops, the counselors, the preachers. Women were told that it was a mark of distinction to be married to a big shot. Maybe they fell for that line, maybe some of them were desperate. For sure many of them were too young to understand.

The motives of the men are easier to see. Some were pursuing what they called love. Some had practicality in mind, help on the farm, that kind of thing. Some marriages were justified as acts of eternal kindness, to give status and companionship in the afterlife to an old woman near death.

Six of Lee's marriages did not work out. One ended in an actual divorce, two ended when the woman went off with another man, one ended when the woman went back to her father's home, one ended because of "misunderstandings," whatever that means, and one ended when Lee rejected the woman because she went away on a trip against his wishes. All of these marriages were short.

Two of his marriages were to elderly women who died soon after, and one was a protective sealing to an orphan who later married one of Lee's sons. Someone should write a novel.

The other ten marriages of John Doyle Lee were stable, long lasting, and apparently successful, though one ended after thirteen years and five children when the wife, Martha Elizabeth Berry, left Lee and married another man, with whom she had an additional six children.

The Loser Sign

November 9, 2005, in the morning, before school, the crazy time just before the bus is to arrive. Chuckie Walker asked Sheila to tie her shoes. The girl was twelve years old, almost thirteen.

Melanie offered Sheila some advice. "Don't tie her shoes," Melanie said. "She should tie her own shoes. She's already spoiled enough."

"Tie your shoes!?" Sheila said. "You can tie your own shoes. But hurry; the bus is almost here."

Chuckie grabbed Sheila's coffee cup from the table. She grabbed the thermos containing the day's supply of coffee.

She headed out the front door, shoe laces flop-flipping, saying, "Then you don't get any more coffee."

The bus was out there, waiting. It comes down the road from the west, and the house is on the north side of the road. The kids have to cross the road in front of the bus and get in on the opposite side. Sheila saw the three of them through the windows of the bus. As she sat down, Chuckie Walker stuck out her tongue at Sheila and gave her the *loser* sign.

After the bus pulled away, Sheila spotted the thermos and the cup of coffee sitting in the dirt across the road where Chuckie had left them.

Two weeks later, in the morning before school, before anyone was out of bed, the telephone rang. Sheila answered. It was Jamie, Chuckie's friend.

"I just want to know how Becky's date went last night," Jamie said.

"Her date?" Sheila paused a moment, thinking. "I'll tell her you called."

Chuckie came down for breakfast. Her shoes seemed to be tied. Sheila said, "How was your date last night?"

"Huh?" said Chuckie.

"Jamie called."

"Oh. I told her I had a date with a high school kid named Johnny Bravo. I told her we were going to Crazy Horse to ride the mechanical bulls." Crazy Horse is a restaurant in New Oxford, a steak place. No mechanical bulls. We eat there sometimes.

"You were home last night," said Sheila. "You watched TV and went to bed early."

"I know," said Chuckie Walker. "I was tricking her."

The *loser* sign: spread the thumb and the forefinger of your right hand so they form a backwards letter *L*. Hold that in front of your forehead and look the loser in the eye.

Robbing the Cradle?

Here is how John Doyle Lee describes three of his marriages in his *Confessions*, his autobiography:

> I baptized a young girl at Readyville, by the name of Sarah
> C. Williams, of rich parentage. She was about ten years
> old, and afterwards emigrated to Nauvoo, with the family
> of Wm. Pace. She was sealed to me in her fourteenth year,
> and is still with me. She is the mother of twelve children,
> and has been a true, faithful, companion to me....
>
> In the spring of 1845 Rachel Andors was sealed to me—
> the woman who has stood by me in all my troubles. A truer
> woman was never born.... I raised her in my family from five
> years of age. She was a sister to my first wife. Her mother,
> Abigail Sheffer, was sealed to me for an eternal state. The
> old lady has long since passed away, and entered into eternal
> rest and joy.

Earlier I talked about the bad side of Mormon polygamy, the
lustful side, the coercive side, the violent side. John Doyle Lee's
marital history might illustrate the good side of Mormon polygamy,
if there is such a thing as a good side.

Ten long-lasting, apparently stable relationships under such a
system would appear to define success. Nine failed relationships
out of nineteen is just under fifty percent, and that is within range
of the divorce rate in America today.

And yet the complacency, the quiet gloating in Lee's account is
disturbing. He remarks on the faithfulness and loyalty of his wives
toward him, but ignores his infidelity toward them.

Most disturbing of all in Lee's account is the underlying hint
of...perhaps I may call it *pedophilia*. Sealing yourself to an old lady
to give her a place in the Mormon heaven is one thing. Marrying
a fourteen-year-old girl whom you baptized when she was ten
or whom you "raised in [your] family from five years of age" is
something else.

I think of Chuckie Walker, who is twelve. I think of Melanie, now
fifteen, and of Crystal, who will soon turn fourteen. I have raised

them from the ages of seven, eight, and nine. I do not have a biological relationship with any of them. Were I religious, perhaps I would baptize them. We do live in the Pond House, so water is available.

But, despite the precedent set by John Doyle Lee, a man I identify with in several ways, I cannot imagine "marrying" these girls, though love them deeply, I do. What would I say to their mother, my only wife? What would she say to me? What would they say? What would I say to myself?

And what would I do if one of them were coerced at an inappropriately early age into marriage by some doctrinaire fundamentalist, even if the marriage were monogamous? Perhaps I would behave in a civilized manner. But what would *I* do? How would the character I call *I* respond to the coercion of his angel?

Serial Matrimonial Monogamy

I have been married three times, I and the character I call *I*. The approach I have followed is serial matrimonial monogamy. Two times marriage did not work out for me, or I did not work out for it. The pattern in both cases went something like this: I married them, and *I* divorced them. *I* was the instigator in both of those divorces.

My first marriage lasted for nineteen years and produced two children. My second marriage lasted for fifteen years and produced no children, though a son from my second wife's first marriage became my stepson. Using the criteria established above, I am tempted to say these marriages were successful, but I know that I would be committing complacency. I would be ignoring the character I call *I*.

Truly, I hate him. Oh, but I love him. I have fought against him and been ruled by him all my life. He is the source of all my trouble and all my glory.

What glory would that be, asshole?

See what I mean? That is how he talks to me, and he talks to me all the time. Believe me, I would kill him if I could. Truly, if I were always *I*, I would absolutely kill him dead.

My third marriage has lasted for five years, and I am stepfather to the three girls that Sheila adopted. It is an excellent marriage, and if it ends, it will not be by my choice. The character I call *I* is still around, but his power may be diminishing.

My failed marriages are the greatest source of sorrow in my life, knock on wood. Divorce is a horrible thing, a mystery, a dark surprise, the worst thing that can happen in a family, except perhaps for the death of a child. No rational person would seek to experience it, though someone like *I* might.

But I have to live with the consequences. In the daylight hours I know that *I* did what I needed to do. The consequences come calling at night, in the darkest hours, the wee hours, the hours of guilt, regret, and self-recrimination. You know the hours I mean; they get longer and worse with age.

Mormon Polygamy: Emma and John Doyle Lee

Emma Lee is my favorite of John Doyle Lee's wives. She is my favorite of all the Mormon women—and, as Wallace Stegner has said, "[the Mormon] women were incredible."

Emma Batchelor married John Doyle Lee in 1858, shortly after the Mountain Meadows Massacre. She stuck with him through all ensuing troubles, including his banishment, his imprisonment, his trial, and his execution. She went with him to Lonely Dell, one of the most God-forsaken places in America. She stayed there alone when he was in jail. She faced down the Navajos and saved the lives of her children. She whipped an insolent prison guard.

She was a strong-willed, self-reliant, independent woman. And yet Juanita Brooks says Emma was satisfied with her role as a polygamous wife:

> Emma…accepted the doctrine of plurality as the highest holiest order of marriage. Everywhere it was being preached and young women came to believe that it was better to bear children to a leader in the church, though he had other wives, than to marry an inferior man. The number of hi

wives and the caliber of his children were something of a measure of a man's worth, a matter of great pride. No man was expected to hold a responsible position in the church who would not live this celestial law.

Juanita Brooks was, in the words of Jan Shipps, "a sometime college English teacher, fulltime Mormon wife and mother, and lifelong resident of Saint George in Utah's southernmost region… [who] made her mark as an historian." In addition to writing two biographies, *Jacob Hamblin: Mormon Apostle to the Indians* and the one on her kinsman John Doyle Lee, she was the editor of *A Mormon Chronicle: The Diaries of John Doyle Lee* and the author of the still standard history, *The Mountain Meadows Massacre*.

Occasionally, I suspect her of romanticism. I take her account of Emma's attitude toward polygamy with a grain of salt. I also take her account of the courtship and marriage of Emma and John Doyle Lee with a grain of salt—at the same time as I am moved by it. Surely love did exist in many polygamous Mormon marriages. Surely this was such a marriage.

I Meet Sheila in Salt Lake City

I was invited to a summer writers' conference in Salt Lake City, as I have said before. Invited because I am an editor, invited to sit on panels and confer with young writers seeking advice on publishing.

Invited to attend readings and talks and a party or two. Invited to give a reading of my own.

A woman approached me one evening before one of the readings. A tall woman, young, sort of blond, maybe a little uneasy. She said her name was Sheila Mulligan, that I had published a story she had written, a story called "Dressing Estelle." I tried to remember the story while saying something nice. She produced a copy of a book I had written and asked if I would sign it. Neither one of us had a pen, so we agreed that I would do that later in the week.

Then she started to walk off. I called her back, asked if she was going to the reading, said maybe we could sit together. Neither one of us much liked the reading, and we may have exchanged a whispered comment or two.

Leaving the auditorium, we were engulfed in the crowd. Someone said hello to me, and I turned away for a moment. When I turned back, Sheila was already disappearing through the crowd.

John Doyle Lee Meets Emma in Salt Lake City

1858, January, four months after the Mountain Meadows Massacre. John Doyle Lee in Salt Lake City, on church business, state business, church and state business, a member of the legislature, representing Washington County. Juanita Brooks:

> There were many long weekends and early adjournments which gave time for pleasure as well as business. Lee visited his daughter, Sarah Jane Dalton, who now lived here; he also courted a new wife. His diary and family legends tell the story.
>
> On his second Sunday night in the city he was called to the stand in the Fourteenth Ward and asked to offer the opening prayer. As the meeting progressed he noticed a fine-looking girl sitting beside a middle-aged woman. He looked straight at her and smiled; she caught his glance and dropped her eyes. At the end of the meeting she disappeared.

Falling in Love with Estelle

Later that evening, after the reading, I remembered the story. Remembered reading it in the car a couple of summers earlier, on a long trip with Jean from Pennsylvania to Oregon and California and Arizona and Mexico and Texas and back home to Pennsylvania

A really good story. Kind of an internal monologue told by a smart overwhelmed, seemingly confused and maybe neurotic, humorous woman narrator. A narrator named Estelle. Yes, I remembered it well

I accepted the story immediately. I wrote a postcard to the author probably a postcard purchased at the Wall Drug Store in Sout

Dakota. I said I loved the story, wanted it for the magazine, an official letter would follow in a couple of weeks. I had been strongly drawn to that woman narrator.

The day after the reading, I ran into Sheila. She told me she had to leave right after the reading. She had a husband and three kids. He was babysitting so she could go to the reading. His parents were visiting from Phoenix. She had to get right home.

I ran into her again the next day. And the day after that. We ran into each other at every turn. She attended my panels. We had coffee together.

The last night of the conference, there was a party. We sat at the edge of a fountain and talked. Maybe for hours. Her husband was there, also a writer. I saw him walking back and forth. I saw him talking to other people.

The conference ended the next day with a final reading. Everyone stood in the lobby afterward, saying good-bye. I said good-bye to Sheila and told her I was staying an extra night to save money on the airfare.

"Well, what will you do tomorrow?"

"I don't know. Just hang around, maybe go shopping."

"We could have lunch," said Sheila.

"Can you get away? I thought you had guests."

"I will pick you up at noon, in that parking lot."

Lunch was good. We talked a lot. She drove me back to the campus, now the empty campus. We walked around and talked.

We sat on a bench. She pulled my book out of her purse, and a pen. This is what I wrote: "Meeting you is the best thing that's happened to me this week—it's been a good week—and besides, I think I am in love with Estelle."

She offered to give me a ride to the airport the next morning.

John Doyle Lee Courts Emma

Still in Salt Lake City, a few days later, the long visit on church business, state business. Juanita Brooks:

The next Wednesday he was invited to attend an evening sociable at the home of his old friend, Brother Dot. Here he met this girl [whom he had noticed at the meeting], Emma Batchelor, lately from England, a lively twenty-two-year-old with a clear complexion, ruddy cheeks, and a delightful accent. He learned that she was working at the home of another friend, Brother Rollins, so the next day he called there and elicited an invitation to dinner.

If he had thought her attractive at first, she seemed doubly so now in her neat dress and white apron…. When he asked for her company to the dance that evening, she blushed to the roots of her hair. He borrowed Brother Stoddard's fine team and closed buggy, secured a soft buffalo robe to go over their knees, and drove her through the snow to the ward house, where he waltzed and schottisched and went through the intricate changes of the quadrille with the ease of much practice.

The next morning he took Emma and Sarah Jane [his daughter] to the city to shop. They were almost the same age, these two, and were as much at home with each other as though they had been sisters. He let them have their pictures taken together; he had his own done too, but alone. He bought each of them a pretty fascinator to go around her shoulders and a lacy handkerchief to carry. He took Sarah Jane home first, for though it was early afternoon, her two children would need her. Nor did he make any other appointments with Emma, but as they rode the last few blocks to Brother Rollins' he put his arm around her and pulled her close, tucking the robe about her.

"Cold?" he asked.

"Not very."

"A pretty girl like you must have had plenty of chance to marry here in Zion."

"A girl doesn't take every chance she gets, though

remember that."

"I will." And he fell into a long silence.

"With you it's different, though," she confessed at last. "You know that night at meeting. I knew you were the one for me as soon as you started to pray. You had such a good voice. Then I opened my eyes and I watched you all the time. I wondered how long it would be before you saw me in the audience. I thought you would; I tried to make you."

"Yes, and you would never look up again. You knew I was smiling at you, and you wouldn't look up. And when it was over, you ran away."

"I guess I was a little scared. I thought maybe you could find me if you really wanted to."

So being assured that Emma would love him and would be willing to cast her lot with him regardless of other wives and children and the life on the frontier, he told her that he would talk it over with President Young and let her know [Young's] decision within a few days.

Love at first sight. A scene straight out of a romance novel: "she blushed to the roots of her hair." How would Juanita Brooks know this? She says that she got her information from family legends and from Lee's diaries.

John Doyle Lee was known for his accurate record keeping: "Andrew Jenson, for many years assistant historian of the Latter-day Saints church, stated many times, that in all his experiences he never saw more accurate or better kept records than those of John Doyle Lee." No doubt Brooks's version closely reflects what Lee wrote about the event. No doubt the romantic feelings were actually his. But Juanita's writing here makes me blush to the roots of my hair.

How Sheila Came to Be Known as "Thumper"

Sheila clomps, which is a way of saying she makes a lot of noise when she walks around the house, on the wooden floors. I guess I could call her Leadfoot, but I call her Thumper instead.

Sometime in the fall of 2001, maybe 2002, we went to Atlantic City, she and I, to walk on the boardwalk from casino to casino, sometimes stopping in the cheesy little stores, sometimes eating hot dogs, funnel cakes, or salt water taffy.

Sheila was wearing boots, her Doc Martens, and she was clomping loudly along beside me on the boardwalk, the sound echoing below. I may have been singing a chorus or two of "Under the Boardwalk," holding hands with my sweetheart.

But there was a rhythm to her clomping, a *ka-thump* kind of rhythm. "Why are you walking like that?" I asked her.

"Like what?" answered Sheila.

"Like in that limping gait. Normally you go *clomp-clomp*, but now you are going *ka-thump, ka-thump*. It's weird, that's all."

"Thank you for noticing," said Sheila. "I have an injured toe."

"An injured toe? Why wasn't I told about this?"

"I didn't think you would care."

"Not care? I turned my life upside down just to be with you! Of course I care. Tell me what happened to your toe."

"I'm not sure, but I think I got stung by a bee."

"Stung by a bee? On your toe? Which toe?"

"My big toe. I think I got stung by a bee on my big toe."

"Right or left big toe?"

"The one on this leg, I think it is my right one."

I looked. She was pointing at her right leg, the one farthest from the ocean. "I am going to have to call you 'Thumper,'" I said. "Because of the noise you are making. You sound like a deformed rabbit."

A Wedding, in the Words of Juanita Brooks

On Tuesday he took Emma in a borrowed carriage to the home of President Young for a personal interview. She had never met this great man personally, so was rather awed at the prospect. Brigham Young held her hand and looked at her searchingly. She met his gaze without flinching, though the natural color deepened in her cheeks and flooded her neck

"So you came with the Martin Company, Sister Batchelor,"
he said after he had invited them to be seated.

"Yes, sir."

"And you have not suffered any permanent effects? Your
feet and ankles didn't get frozen?"

"I was always one of the first to wade the streams," she
said, "but I took off my shoes and stockings and carried
them across, so I could have them dry afterwards. And I
always scrubbed my feet hard with my wool neck piece.
And I asked the Dear Lord to help me take care of myself,
since there was no one else to look after me, and promised
that if I should come through whole, I'd not complain at
my lot, no matter what it was."

"But you were sealed to Brother Kippen, weren't you?
Have you not complained at that?"

"That was something different. I was sent to his house
to live, and I earned all I got by washing and ironing and
scrubbing and waiting on the first wife. I was as a servant
maid to her. I thought that the sealing was as a protection
to give me a home, and then I could choose my husband."

"And do you think that you have found the man you
want now?"

"Oh, yes, sir."

"You understand the order of this kingdom. You know
that he has other wives, and you are willing to take your
place among them?"

"Yes, sir."

Brigham rose and took her hand, motioning for her to
stand also.

"Sister Emma, I bless you in the name of the Lord. You
are free from any bonds with any man previous to this hour.
You will find Brother Lee a kind husband, who does not
expect any one woman to be subservient to another, but
each to have her own place as a wife by his side. Be faithful

to him through all adversity and you will find him a pilla
of strength to you. Make your preparations and meet u
here at 12 o'clock tomorrow noon, and we will perform
the ceremony."

So it was that on January 7, Emma Bachelor was sealed t
John D. Lee in Brigham Young's own sealing room. After th
ceremony he took her to his boarding place at Brother Ezr
T. Benson's and introduced her to the other members of th
legislature who also ate there. Sister Benson had prepare
and decorated a wedding cake. John D. brought some cherr
brandy and other liquors in honor of the occasion, and the
celebrated with a fine dinner.

Maybe it worked out this way. Probably Brigham explained th
obligations of a polygamous wife. Maybe Emma accepted them al
Maybe it was all just this ordinary and everyday. I know nothin
that would allow me to doubt it.

And the marriage lasted until the end, until Lee's death. Emma
loyalty never wavered, her commitment to John Doyle Lee.

Another Wedding

Sheila's divorce came through quickly. Not smoothly, not happily
but quickly, before the new family left Salt Lake City and move
into the Pond House in Pennsylvania.

My divorce took two more years, unpleasant years, contentiou
years.

The wedding took place on the nineteenth of June, 2002, in th
courtroom of Judge Kuhn. A civil ceremony, attended and witnesse
by the kids. We took pictures at the Grotto of Saint Mary Seaton
down in Emmitsburg, Maryland. We went out for dinner.

Two months later we had our friends over for a party. I bough
a keg of beer, a bottle of gin, and a jug of wine in honor of th
occasion. A caterer served Indian food. Many children played o
the lawn, the lawn of the Pond House.

In the Grotto after the Wedding

From Genesis to Redemption

It started in Salt Lake City, what you are reading now. I left my wife, and I went to Salt Lake City. By way of Mexico. I knew that my next wife was waiting for me there, in Salt Lake City. One subject of the essay is the family that ensued. It is an ongoing story.

The other subject is the story of John Doyle Lee. While I was living in Salt Lake City, I had a little apartment, and every morning I would read the newspaper. One week the newspaper published a series of articles on the Mountain Meadows Massacre. The author was noncommittal about the role of the church fathers in the massacre, about the role of John Doyle Lee. They may have been innocent, he may have been guilty. The articles were pretty dumb, to tell you the truth.

So I went looking for a book. I found *The Mountain Meadows Massacre* by Juanita Brooks, and that book led to other books, to Fawn Brodie's biography of Joseph Smith, to the Mormon books of Wallace Stegner, to books about the Great Salt Lake, about the geography of the Great Basin, about the exploration of the American West, about the Mormon migration, to biographies of Brigham Young, Orrin Porter Rockwell, John Cooke Bennett, other Mormon luminaries and non-luminaries, and to Juanita Brooks's biography of her kinsman, John Doyle Lee.

My kinsman too. No, not in any real or literal sense. A spiritual sense, a connection on the basis of character, character and experience. When I came upon the life and history of John Doyle Lee, I was feeling reviled. Because I had left my wife, because many friends did not understand, because stories were told that were not true stories that became gossip, then gospel. Or so it seemed to me.

John Doyle Lee was reviled. Because of the Mountain Meadow Massacre; because of stories that were told, stories that were not true, stories that became gospel. And he was a difficult man, John Doyle Lee, a man with a complex personality. I think he was character with an *I*, himself and a character named *I*. People talked about him, kept an eye on him. His character worked against him his strong convictions, his sense of right and wrong, his silence, his intelligence, his many talents, his success, his pride, his hauteur, his bullheadedness. Juanita Brooks:

> One who reads from his writings, or the writings of his contemporaries, might conclude that Lee was a gifted and intelligent man, generous and kindly, but egotistical and apt to be dictatorial.... He was...either ardently loved or heartily disliked.

After the massacre Lee increasingly became a mythological personage, a heartless murderer, a fiend. The massacre was a mistake. Everyone knew that immediately, even the perps, most of whom ran away. But he stayed. John Doyle Lee stayed behind—out of pride, out of a naive conviction that his innocence, his status, his success, his talent, his intelligence, his basic goodness, his generosity, would protect him.

They did not. The entire blame for the Mountain Meadows Massacre came down on his head. He was the only one they could blame. Everyone was guilty, the men who did it, the community that wanted it, the big shots—the bishops, the preachers, the counselors, Brigham Young, the church itself—even the victims who came into Utah and taunted the Mormons at the very moment the Mormons were convinced they were under attack from the east. All of them were guilty. And all of them were innocent. The logic is inescapable. If everyone was guilty, then everyone was innocent. Every last one of them.

But one man could be blamed, the scapegoat, John Doyle Lee, tried, found guilty, condemned, and killed.

Years went by, and a miracle occurred. They figured it out, the Church of Jesus Christ of Latter-day Saints figured it out. Thanks to time, to calmer heads, to the hard work of Juanita Brooks, the church finally figured it out and reversed its decision.

They could not abort the trial, could not stop the firing squad, could not deflect the bullets, could not raise John Doyle Lee from his murderer's grave. So they decided to resurrect his soul instead.

Jan Shipps wrote the introduction to the reprint of Juanita Brooks's book on the massacre, the valedictory printing I want to call it, the printing that was released just months after the action described by Jan Shipps took place:

> Juanita Brooks's research made enough facts available to the First Presidency and the Council of the Twelve Apostles of the LDS church for them to act on April 20, 1961, to authorize John D. Lee's "reinstatement to membership and former blessings," a consummation that had been devoutly wished by his family and descendents since his disgrace [and church-sponsored execution] nearly a century before.
>
> *John Doyle Lee 1812–1871*
> *May He Rest in Peace.*

Acknowledgments

Many people assisted me during the writing and rewriting and rewriting of this book. Some of the essays contained herein were originally published in different form in the "Editor's Pages" section of *The Gettysburg Review*; this project would never have been begun nor proceeded to fruition without the able editorial assistance of Mark Drew, Mindy Wilson, and Kim Dana Kupperman. Many readers over the years have offered valuable suggestions and guidance, among them Carol Frost, Richard Frost, Fritz Gaenslen, Fred Leebron, Sheila Mulligan, Lorin Rees, Kathryn Rhett, Jack Ryan, Philip Schultz, Michael Waters, Alison Wellford, Paul Zimmer, and many others whom I am embarrassed to have forgotten. For technical assistance above and beyond the call of duty, I thank Brandon Cornwell and Libby Howard. Without the extraordinary support of Hope Maxwell Snyder, however, there would never have been an actual book, and to her I am especially grateful. The four persons to whom I owe the most, my deepest thanks and enduring love, are those mentioned in my dedication.